A Hope
and a
Future

© 2006
By Marsha N Woods

ISBN 0-9779334-2-3

Foreword by Nathan Tasker

It is no small feat to look back over your life and share the details of your journey with others. It becomes increasingly more difficult the more twists and turns you add in- but so much more beautiful and engaging for the reader!

Nicki's story is one of remarkable beginnings, distant lands, and the importance of finding a "home". However, it is really more than Nicki's story that you hold in your hands. It is God's story. One He desires to invite us all to participate in. And not just as friends or companions.

As family.

Nicki' story is one of grace and mercy, experienced at the hands of Tony and Marsha, her adoptive parents. To be taken in and shown love is a story I will never tire of hearing. Nicki's real life experience of this love that allows for new beginnings and second chances, leads her to share of her adoption into a much larger family, the family of God.

"How great is the love the Father has lavished on us, that we should be called children of God!" (1 John 3:1)

With impressive insight for her years, and an honesty that grips your heart and demands that this story be heard, Nicki's journey will call you to see the sovereign hand of God in all that we take for granted. I trust that this story will help you to view your own story with greater clarity. I pray that it will remind you, as it did me, of a hope and a future that awaits all who would pray, "Our Heavenly Father".

Blessings,

Nathan

Prologue

*J*t was early in the morning of the 9th of August 1989. Tony Woods sat on the front porch of a rustic old cabin and looked out over Lake Nojiri, in western Japan. Life was good, he thought to himself as he set aside his steaming cup of coffee and opened up his Bible in preparation for his daily routine of reading and contemplating what God might be doing in his life. He and his wife Marsha had been serving as missionaries in Japan for over ten years, raising their two boys, Trevor and Nathan to love the Lord and to love the country and the people to whom they'd been sent. He watched the sun slowly appear over the lake, a huge red ball of fire lighting up the water below. Tony marveled at how it always seemed to resemble Japan's "rising sun" national symbol.

As he opened his new "Through the Year" Bible that he had just bought, he thought to himself how glad that he had been introduced to this Bible reading guide by a fellow missionary. Before, he had just read the Bible, but this daily style seemed to be a little easier to settle into. Today's reading was from the book of Jeremiah, and the passage he noticed was Jeremiah 29:11.

"Not bad, " he thought to himself, taking his red pen and underlining the verse, then noting the year in the margin. Of course, he had no way of knowing, but at that very moment in a small town in southern Russia his daughter was being born: a girl he would not meet until she had passed her third birthday. Neither did he know that in the three years to follow, he and Marsha would walk through the darkest valley of their lives, as their oldest son, Trevor, succumbed to a brief but horrific bout with leukemia at the age of 16. It would not be until fours years later that Tony would return to that passage of scripture and be reminded of God's Hand upon him: a Hand that gives and takes away.

"For I know the plans I have for you declares the Lord, plans to protect you and not to harm you, plans to give you a hope and a future". Jeremiah 29:11

"For I know the plans I have for you declares the Lord, plans to protect you and not to harm you, plans to give you a hope and a future". Jeremiah 29:11

Chapter One

Arrival

*W*e imagine that the baby's mother was a beautiful young dark eyed Armenian girl, possibly a survivor of the Great Spitak Earthquake, December 7th, 1988, which would kill nearly one out of every four of her countrymen in a single horrifying moment. No one knows how she managed to leave her hometown and find her way to Armivir, a Russian village of about 150,000, just a few miles north of the Georgian border. Nor is it known how she located the small

1

state-run orphanage and made arrangements to leave her precious 2kg or 4.4lb newborn daughter in their care.   The letter she left behind said only that she loved her daughter dearly, but was unable to care for her. Fortunately, the letter was not all that she left. She also left the baby with a name: Maria, after Mary the mother of Jesus, and testimony of her Coptic Orthodox upbringing. The Russian caretakers who accepted the child began calling her by the term of endearment common to that area, adding "sha" to the shortened Maria, or Ma, making her name "Ma-sha," as if to say, "cute little Mary".

The head of the orphanage was a remarkable doctor by the name of "Vegislav," a man who had devoted his life to seeing every child under his care find the best possible future. Many of the children who came through his doors were victims of neglect, abuse and physical abnormality. Some were born to parents who had used drugs, which all but destroyed their chances of finding homes where they would be loved and properly cared for. For these children, Dr. Vegislav did the best he could with the pitifully small resources he had to work with. Without a doubt, he loved each and every one of his children.

But one child caught his heart in a special way. Perhaps it was her eyes that drew him to her. They were crossed, a condition known as Strabismus, and in that country unfortunately it was a condition that could not be easily fixed. Quite often people would exercise pejorative superstitions against such a condition, calling it a sign of retardation, or worse yet, the 'evil eye'. Fortunately, Dr. Vegislav knew that Strabismus is a simple physical condition where the muscles that turn the eye are just a bit too long, so that they tend to reel out of control when the brain sends the signal to turn the eyes. He knew that behind those eyes dwelt the heart of a very special and intelligent child. He knew as well that her mother had been a 'good girl' who had never taken drugs and was clean and honest.

Masha must have known that Dr. Vegislav believed in her as well, because a bond existed between them like no other. Evidently to be called to the good Dr.'s office was a special treat for the children and usually meant a reward of a 'yablushka' or small worm eaten apple.

Because of his love for little 'Masha', three years later Dr. Vegislav sat in his office tortured by his thoughts and uncertain what to do. His orphanage was a maternity orphanage and existed by the meager subsidy of the

Russian government. One outfit of basic clothing and subsistence food was provided, as well as a bare bones upkeep of the facility, which was a small but clean renovated home on the edge of town. But the subsidy came with conditions, and they expressly stipulated that child support was only given to children up to the age of three. If the orphanage had not succeeded in placing a child by that time, then other sources would have to be utilized.

The doctor scoffed out loud at that. What 'other sources' could there possibly be for a child who had already passed her third birthday, with no parents, no family and no place to go? The options were so repulsive he dared not dwell on them, but gazed outside instead. On the playground, he spotted little Masha, running and laughing with the other children. Two months had gone by since her third birthday, and soon he would have no choice but to turn her out. What will become of her? he thought to himself.

His thoughts were interrupted by the ringing of the telephone. That in itself was occasion for surprise, since the phones rarely ever worked. But even more surprising were the woman's words he heard when he answered. "Hello. My name is Alla, and I represent an

American couple here in Moscow who are seeking to adopt a child."

"Moscow?" Dr. Vegislav could not remember the last time a call had come in from so far away. And what was it they were saying? Americans? Looking for a child to adopt?

Before he could even reply, Alla was voicing his own concerns over the phone. "I know that the government does not normally adopt to foreigners, and I know too that such a thing is next to impossible. I just had to call and see if …"

The doctor interrupted her, "There is a child, a three year old girl. Tell the Americans that if they will come to Armivir, I will do everything in my power to make it possible."

Back in Moscow, the couple had begun packing to leave. After a week of fruitless searches throughout the city, they had come to the conclusion that what they sought was indeed impossible. Several dead end 'leads' and a couple of just plain dishonest 'deals' had been offered, leading them to understand that there was just no hope in Moscow, even though they'd been led to believe that there were hundreds of orphans just waiting for them. Now they were discouraged and defeated, remembering the past year as they had watched their firstborn, Trevor, die of a rare and untreatable form of Leukemia. He had suffered stoically for eight months, and then left them behind with a grief that would not be healed easily.

The decision to adopt one more child was not a sudden one; Tony and Marsha had been "in the adoption market" so to speak, for several years following the loss of their unborn child while serving as missionaries in West Africa. The adoption of their son, Nathan had been a highlight when he had miraculously come into their lives, after about 4 years of trying many different avenues. He brought with himself, five years earlier, a joy only paralleled by the birth of Trevor, and as soon as Nathan was a couple of years old, Tony and Marsha, as well as Trevor and Nathan, knew there was room in their hearts for another child, if only they could adopt one more.

Adoption had become more difficult since Nathan, and year after year, they were turned back. Finally Trevor was 16 and Nathan was 11, and they'd all about given up on the 'one more' campaign. However, now Trevor was gone and the family began to think again. In the summer of 1992, a niece, hearing of Tony and Marsha's desire to adopt, had located a 'friend of a friend' who was Russian living in Denver, Colorado. When contacted, she had promised that there were over 100,000 orphans just 'waiting to be picked up' in Russia.

After a lot of prayer and paperwork, plus a sizeable chunk of money handed over to her, this trip to Russia had been a last desperate attempt, and it soon became apparent that it had indeed been a futile, yet costly one as well. Perhaps, they thought, some things evidently were just not meant to be.

But as they would soon learn, some things were also *meant* to be. Alla, a friend of the woman in Denver, had been commandeered into helping Tony and Marsha in Moscow. She spoke not a word of English and didn't seem to have any discernible personality, but she was a woman with a mission, and had begun, after the last disappointment in Moscow, to call all over Russia looking for an orphan.

After a few days, she came to Tony and Marsha with the news of her fruitful conversation with the people in Armivir. "There is a girl in an orphanage nearly two thousand miles south of Moscow, and the doctor in charge, a Dr. Vegislav has promised to help us to the best of his ability if we will only come."

They began to protest, speaking out of their discouragement, saying that it was too far to go, they had no more time or money, and with so little to go on it might be another ruse ... but Alla added the fact that would put all indecision to rest. "Her name is Marsha."

"You know we have to go, don't you?" Tony said quietly.

"Absolutely," Marsha agreed.

Think about it

I guess I'll never know how everything worked together to bring my parents to Dr. Vegislov and me, except that it was a whole lot of miracles that only God could have put together. What do you think God is doing in your life right now that will affect your future?

"Ask and it will be given to you; seek and you will find; knock and the door will be opened to you."

Luke 11:9

Chapter 2

Finding ME

𝔗he flight to Krasnador was not to be forgotten. In the crumbling Soviet Union, tickets for Soviet citizens were only about five dollars, but you must remember that that was about half of a middle class worker's monthly salary. However, a foreigner had to pay about a HUNDRED dollars for a ticket to Krasnador which was about 1500 miles from Moscow.

Tony, Marsha, Alla and Nadia, the translator went to

the airport, struggled out onto the runway with the large boxes of clothes that they had brought for the orphanage and were greeted at the stairs by several very unhappy Russians who were obviously disembarking. It was explained that they had been thrown off the airplane to make room for the more expensive seats!

Marsha struggled up the stairs with the large box of clothes she had brought for the orphanage and tripped a few times on the front of her long coat. Her mother had given it to her when she left the States on a premonition that it might come in handy. As it turned out, because of the brisk Russian autumn, she basically had it on for about a month straight!

At any rate, stumbling up the steps, dropping the box a few times, and being subjected to the scolding of the attendants for being weak, all in all made for a rather a dramatic entrance. As soon as she reached the top stair, the box was wrenched from her arms was stowed in what is generally thought of as 'first class'. Marsha thought bemusedly that supposedly in the equality of comrade-ness, first class had evidently become the cargo section. Marsha, divested of her load, took a deep breath and looked up to see a very portly stewardess pointing gruffly to an empty seat.

As she sat down, the woman sitting in the next seat glared at her and pointed to the seat and to her wedding ring and looked anxiously out the window. Marsha could only surmise that the husband had been one of the deportees. Having no Russian skills, she just bowed and looked sad as she reached for her seat belt. She wished she had Tony nearby for this trip, but he, as well as Alla and Natasha had been told to go to other seats and had disappeared into the back somewhere. Finding no seat belt, she leaned back and discovered that the seat was broken as well as it continued to lean back indefinitely, so she sat up straight and began to pray............

When finally they arrived unscathed in Krasnador, the capital city, Tony and Marsha met together with the translator. Their next step would be to get a taxi.

"Whatever happens, do not speak," said Nadia. "It could quadruple the price".

The handy thing of looking like a white Russian was that if you said nothing, no one knew you were a foreigner. Fortunately, within a few minutes a taxi was contracted for the three hour drive to Armivir. By now it was very late and very dark, and they wondered about the road worthiness of the taxi. As they headed out of the airport, the car began to wobble and weave on the road, and it was ascertained that there was a problem with the tire. Sure enough, it was very flat. "No problem," they thought, "just a little time delay."

Actually, it was soon to be revealed that the driver had in fact, NO spare tire. Back to the airport they wobbled, only to watch him bargain and beg with the other drivers till a nice bald tire was procured and they were on their way again.

Into the night they careened on the lonely road. For three hours seldom a car was met, and either out of self preservation or exhaustion, the four passengers slouched down in their coats, while trying to brace themselves for safety, and went to sleep. Eventually, they arrived without further incident into a small country town. They drove right to the orphanage and were delighted to see several people standing outside the gate with flashlights in their hands.

As they pulled up to the gate, the other back tire hissed down into a flat, but they were too overjoyed at arriving to give much thought to the taxi driver's dilemma. After all, he was now in town and could probably find someone to help him.

Quickly they were ushered into a warm and brightly lit building. It was obviously the clinic and a warm fire burned in the corner. Over tea, Dr. Vegislav welcomed them and explained that Masha was of Armenian extraction although her father had been a white Russian. They were anxious to see the child but were told that no one was allowed to interrupt her sleep, and tomorrow would come soon enough.

As they had neared the village an hour before, Marsha mentioned to Tony that they had no idea where they would find to stay at this late hour. Tony worried that they might have to sleep on the floor of the orphanage, to which Marsha laughed, "Well, I guess if it's been good enough for 'my daughter' for the past three years......."

You can imagine their relief to be taken by the orphanage van to the one and only hotel in town, where Dr. Vegislav had made reservations for two rooms. It was a building of several stories and several rooms, all with adjoining toilets, albeit none with any seats. It was also noted that the telephones were made in amusing multicolored plastic, resembling a child's toy, but actually didn't work anyway. There was no hot water, nor was there heat in the rooms or lighting in the halls. It was explained by Nadia that all of these 'amenities' that we take for granted had fallen victim to the shortages that plagued Russia at that time.

The rooms looked wonderful to the exhausted travelers. They said their good nights to each other and each settled into their respective twin beds (which were nailed to the opposite walls of the room for whatever reason). Then began the long and somewhat fitfull night trying to get warm and at the same time relax while fully clothed, including their coats.

Morning did come, and they awoke to find a picturesque little country town. The streets were lined with old trees and the stately buildings spoke of better days. There was a large statue of Lenin in the town square, which made Nadia and Alla laugh, saying that the people in this town did not yet know that Lenin was dead and his "Great Experiment" was in tatters under a crumbling government. They ate a small breakfast of bread and cheese and headed out to the orphanage.

Think about it:

My parents wanted to complain about the discomforts they met on the way to find me: airplanes that were WAY beyond their "due date", slick tires on taxis, colorful phones which never worked and a total lack of toilet seats, to name a few. But then Mom said it well, "I guess if it's been good enough for my daughter, then it's good enough for me." And when you think about it, it WAS good enough. I never missed those things as a three year old, because I'd never been exposed to them. What things in your life do you really think you need, and is it because you need them or because someone has shown them to you? How about we try and be happy with what we have?

Live as children of the light.....
and find out what pleases the Lord....

Ephesians 5:8

Chapter Three

Choosing Me

*M*y Dad always tells the story of the first time he saw me. I was having a music lesson, as we did every day at the orphanage. This morning, since it was October and the leaves were turning gold and falling, we were all instructed to dance around to the music while picking up paper leaves as gracefully as we could. When Dad walked into the room, I had my back to him, intent on picking up as many leaves as anyone else, but he says even though he couldn't see my eyes and know it was

16

me, he saw a light shining down on my head, lighting up the room. My Mom said, "He whispered under his breath,'"Oh yes!' and we knew our search was over!"

The process began that day and would continue for the next week. Officials were visited, papers were filled out, assurances were made and each day brought them closer to the goal, one painful step at a time. In almost every instance, discussions would begin with, "This is an impossible thing you are asking, we cannot do this." But without wavering, more visits were made, followed by return calls to the first officials.

Often they said, "The man in the other department said he would do this if you will," and the first official would consider a moment and reply, "Well, OK, but only if *he* will!" Then it was back to the second official with assurances that the other man would do it if this one did.

It began to take on an almost comical tone, if it hadn't been so important. One lady said the whole deal was off, because of something that wasn't done properly clear back in the United States! They thought they would surely fail this time, but as Tony and Marsha stood by and mutely prayed, she picked up the phone,

MIRACULOUSLY got through to Moscow, and the whole problem was solved.

During all this time of bureaucratic maneuvering, Tony and Marsha helped wherever they could, but for the most part just tried to stay out of the way and be inconspicuous. Nadia told them to remain out of sight until they could see what reactions Dr. Vegislav received from the official community in town.

If they did leave the hotel on their own, it was only to walk and look, never to speak, lest word got out that "Amerikanskis" were in town. They enjoyed the beauty of the old styled streets, but were dismayed to see so much poverty by people who obviously were very refined and educated.

All along the sidewalk, men and women would stand silently, a few household items or war medals lying at their feet, for sale to the highest bidder. Every shop that had anything to offer was lined up with people hoping to purchase daily necessities.

Walking past a bakery, Tony saw the long line, then stepped up to the window and peered inside to see what they were selling. It looked like small loaves of black bread which smelled wonderful, but as he had to play the mute, and didn't have any money anyway, he wouldn't be buying any today.

As he stepped back from the window, a man in line called out to him in Russian, obviously asking a question. Tony didn't understand him and was vowed to silence anyway, so he just shrugged his shoulders in reply. The man threw up his hands and wailed out a lament, walking away in despair. Imagine Tony's chagrin to see the whole line breaking up and people trudging off resignedly!

Every day when all the requisite trips to offices with all their paperwork and attempted phone calls were finished, the four foreigners to Armivir, Tony Marsha Nadia and Alla would meet in one of the two hotel rooms and play cards and eat salami and cheese that they had brought from Moscow. The stakes were high in this card game. The winners got squares of much coveted and also imported from Moscow....., toilet paper! It was really great fun and the Russian girls had an aplomb about the whole shortage issue that impressed Tony and Marsha. When the toilet paper was gone, Nadia said pragmatically, "Oh, we'll get something tomorrow at the black market". Upon investigation, there was no toilet paper to be had, so Nadia shrugged her shoulders and bought some rather nice linen stationery.

"Are we going to write thank you letters to all the offices?" Marsha innocently asked.

"Oh no, this will be our toilet paper now," came the answer. Marsha wondered how much longer her toilet would be functioning with attitudes like this.

Another day in the market they came across some wafer type cookies and decided to treat all 60 orphanage children to a cookie apiece. "Absolutely not," came the reply from Dr. Vegislav. "We have no idea where these cookies were made and how long they've sat around unrefrigerated, so 'my' children are not having them." With a bit of awe and respect, the cookies were added to the nightly cheese and salami meals.

After about a week, it appeared that the adoption papers would indeed be granted. By now as well, news was leaking out that there was an American couple in town and that they were involved with the local orphanage. Finally, a reporter visited the orphanage and learned the truth. Tony and Marsha began to fear for the success of their venture if the townspeople responded negatively, but to their great surprise and relief, a wave of approval was heard, even resulting in the local radio station coming to do an interview of the lucky couple. As the sound crew set up in Dr. Vegislav's office, under the watchful stare of a portrait of Stalin, Tony asked Nadia what was appropriate to say. "Just tell the truth" she answered. "Russians will know if you are lying".

The interviewer began with a simple statement. "Mr. and Mrs. Woods," he said through Nadia, "you are to be commended for this wonderful thing you are doing. We have heard of the loss of your son, and our hearts hurt with yours." Then he asked, "How will you raise this child, when you take her back home?" Tony thought for a moment, said a silent prayer and launched into a story.

"There was a book a few years ago called 'Peace Child,' a true story written by a Christian missionary named Don Richardson. It tells of his struggle to settle a dispute between two warring headhunter tribes in New Guinea. When peace agreements were finally completed, the tribes exchanged newborn babies. Each tribe promised to raise the other tribe's baby as one of their own, a symbol of the trust between the two.

He went on to compare that 'Peace Child' with Jesus Christ, the Son of God, who came to man as a helpless child but succeeded in bringing the way for perfect peace for all people." He paused for the translator and then continued. "Little Masha is like our Peace Child," he explained. "We will take her to our home. We will watch over her and care for her as best we can. And we will teach her about her beginnings and help her to understand all you have done for her. We will also teach her about the love of Jesus, Who has made all this possible today."

Well at least that's how I imagine that it happened. All I know until that time is what I've been told, and the story has been lovingly told again and again until I can see it in my memory as clearly as if I were there, which, when you think of it, I guess I was!

Think about it:

When it came right down to it, my Dad decided to follow Nadia's advice and just "tell the truth", including his conviction that all this had come about because of Jesus. He was surprised and overjoyed to discover that the Russian people who heard his story were thrilled, and wanted to know more about Christianity. Have you ever been tempted to "water down" your story because you're afraid of what people will think? I can tell you right now, it's always better to "just tell the truth". You'll feel better for it, and God will be able use your real story a lot better than a made up one.

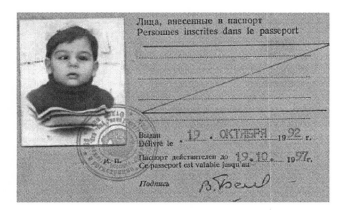

*The Lord will watch over your coming and going both
now and forevermore.*

Psalms 121:8

Chapter Four

Leaving Home

*N*ow that I was really and finally adopted, the next
stop was to the photo studio for a passport picture.
This was the first time I had ever been outside the
orphanage, and seeing a real car for the first time, I
cried out "Machinka!" (car!). Marsha, (my new mom),
the translator and the photographer all tried very hard
to put a bow in my hair for the picture, but with the
short "orphanage cut", it was almost impossible. They
finally stuck it on with tape, and I smiled so big it made

24

everyone in the shop laugh. Of course, as is the case with any three year old, by the time the camera was ready to snap the photo, I was bored and wanted to be done and off the stool, so you'll see that I'm no longer smiling in the photo. As with so many of God's perfect plans, the petulant look on the photo actually helped me get out of the country, because I needed to be not only cross- eyed, but a little 'delayed' to fit the criteria for adoption, and that picture certainly conveyed the look I needed! As soon as the camera snapped and the picture was produced, I returned to my cheerful adventurous self for the ride back to the orphanage. Little did I know what lay ahead, that my world would be turned upside down and I would not be the carefree little laughing girl again for many more weeks..

Early the next morning, we had to leave before daylight to make the drive to Krasnador, and then fly to Moscow. I was awakened before the other kids, so that I could leave without upsetting them. I was told later that I was shouting "I'm going to America! I'm going to America!" If the ride in the 'machinka' to the photo shop was anything like 'going to America', I was all for it! I was excited at so many levels I could hardly contain myself! I had new clothes that I received from my new mom and dad, including a beautiful blue jacket. As it was bitter cold in the predawn morning, one of the nurses struggled with my excited gestures to help me put on my coat. My new Dad reached out to help, but she pulled me away, and with big tears in her eyes explained to the translator,

"Let me do this just one more time." Then my new mom started to cry as all the nurses gave me huge bear hugs and smothered me with kisses. The tears must have clued me into the fact that this 'America' must be different than the photo shop, because right then and there I started to grieve, not even knowing what was happening.

All the way to Krasnador, I sat quietly in the lap of the woman who had become my mother. I looked out the window. "Where were we going?" I wondered. "Where are my teachers, and Dr. Vegislav and all my friends?" Except for the trip to the photo shop, I had never been anywhere. Now, we seemed to travel for hours, with nothing to do and no one familiar in sight. For the first time, I began to feel a little afraid.

Arriving at the Krasnador airport after a three hour drive from Armivir, they were told that in spite of four reserved tickets, there was only one seat available. One person could go right away, but the others would have to wait three days until the next available flight. There was much discussion but they all agreed that little Masha needed to get to a safe and distant environment as soon as possible, so it was decided that Tony, being the only man, would take Little Masha, leaving Marsha (who was more and more being called 'Big Marsha', a term she didn't particularly like), Nadia the translator and Alla, to wait behind.

As Tony, rather nervously holding his new daughter got on the plane; Masha started babbling in Russian, using the word "Mama!" a lot. Tony was sure he was up for this adventure, but nevertheless, riding a very substandard airplane with a three year old getting more and more agitated about sitting on your lap wasn't too inviting. Soon, he thought of a ploy, and pulled out a business card, handed it to me and said "Mama!". Who knows what I was thinking, but I settled right down and clutched the card all the way to Moscow. Sure enough, as everyone knew, Tony was the right man for the job.

He was gentle, but firm. He wouldn't let me get off of his lap and run around the airplane, which bothered me considerably, but when I gave up struggling, he held me close and sang softly in my ear. I had never heard Christian hymns before, and I sat quietly all the way to Moscow, clutching a card with the promise of "Mama" and wondering what this wonderful thing was that I was hearing.

In Moscow, the problems got complicated again as Marsha, Alla and the translator finally made it back three days later. There was the matter of getting a visa to get into America, but first, they would need to go to the Russian Immigration office for little Masha's travel papers that would enable her to get OUT of Russia. There, unbelievably, they were told that Masha's new passport that had been granted in Krasnador, was only good for domestic travel, and that she could not leave the country!

Tony, Marsha and Nadia slumped down in the waiting room in a definite state of confusion. What should they do? It seemed that their only option was to return to Krasnador on that dreadful airplane and start over. They couldn't think of anything worse, and were discussing whether they had the nerve or energy to do that again.

While they were trying to find the courage and energy

to go back to Krasnador, as well as trying to think of what, if any, their other options might be, a faint hope of rescue came from a place they never expected: the driver, a man named Vitali.

The "friend of a friend" who had arranged Tony and Marsha's trip from America had hired Vitali, presumably sight unseen, for ten dollars a day. His job would be to drive them around Moscow in his private car as they visited orphanages. No one knew how the lady in America was able to find this man, but although he said he normally worked for the military, he was happy to take time off to help us.

Something was suspicious about him from the beginning. He apparently spoke no English but 'talked' to us thru Nadia the translator. They thought his taking off work was a generous gesture, but we must remember at that time, the average Russian was making ten dollars A MONTH, so this was good money he was earning. Tony and Marsha thought it was strange that every time he parked the car he removed the windshield wipers and locked them inside the trunk, but they relaxed when they saw others doing the same thing. Again, because of the economy, 'things' must be guarded carefully from petty thieves.

However, from the first day, it was clear that he had some special clout with the police. He got stopped several times a day, usually for minor traffic infractions, but also because he never paid much attention to road signs, doing whatever he wanted, driving wherever he wished, speeding when it seemed possible or interesting. It's rather alarming to be stopped by a policeman who's brandishing an AK47, but whenever the police would come up to him, he would show them his identification card, and they would just turn and walk away. Once they just looked in the window and walked away! Both the translator Nadia, as well as Alla were increasingly afraid of him and suspected that he was deep into the KGB. They always cautioned Tony and Marsha to be very careful around him, even to refrain from speaking English within earshot of him, as they were growing suspicious of what he did and didn't know. Often they wished aloud that they had some other recourse than using him as a driver, but in 1992, there were very few private automobiles in Moscow, and he would have to do.

Ironically, on that fateful day, as the group slumped in the immigration office digesting the news that the passport was no good, and they might indeed have to retrace their steps to Krasnador, they were once again

30

surprised to find God can even use a KGB operative! Just as Tony and Marsha were about to despair, Vitali asked the translator what the problem was. She explained the situation of the inferior passport, and he jumped up out of his seat, grabbed the stack of documents and said, "Just moment." Then he walked right through, without knocking, the big leather doors of the main office. Nadia slumped into a chair and said, "Now we're finished, he'll surely get us arrested or worse!"

They all shivered in silence while Tony and Marsha prayed, and secretly wondered if they were prepared to live in the gulag. However, in just a few minutes, Vitali came bounding out of the office, laughing and smiling with a man in a suit, who was very friendly and solicitously asked them if they would like tea. They nodded numbly, and within minutes this official had an elaborate tea set sent out, resplendent with hot drinks and exquisite sweets. They timidly helped themselves and in within thirty minutes they had a beautiful new passport good for international travel!

As soon as the good byes were said and the group of stunned petitioners left the building, clutching the new passport, Tony said to the driver, "Vitali, how did you do that?"

"Oh, was simple," he said, with gestures and very broken English. "I show man my card, say you my BOSS living in America!"

Think about it:

Have you ever felt that just living in this world is too big a challenge to put up with? Well I have. There have been plenty of times when things pile up around me, and I just think, "Enough!" But when those times come, I remember the story of my adoption, and the way God used people who didn't even know they were being used. And I remember how my Mom and Dad never gave up, even when the rest of the world was saying, "Impossible!" But not only was it possible, it was all part of God's plan for my life. And nothing could stop it: not Russian bureaucrats, not embassy paper pushers, not even thousands of miles with no apparent way of communicating. And you know what? God has a plan for you, too. And He's going to see to it that His plan gets carried out. What did the Apostle Paul write to the Philippians? "…being confident of this, that he who began a good work in you will carry it on to completion until the day of Christ Jesus." (Philippians 1:6). I believe that. Do you?

"Ask and it will be given to you; seek and you will find; knock and the door will be opened to you."

Luke 11:9

Chapter 5

Leaving

*A*s soon as Tony and Marsha, Nadia and Alla were back at the apartment and away from Vitali, they roared with laughter! Who would believe that a government office would grant a new passport based on the fact that Tony was a 'sleeper' working for the KGB! How hilarious are the ways of man and the ingenuity of God! As they were soon to learn, however, those ways would still be tested.

After the Russians had finally provided everything Tony and Marsha and little Masha needed to leave the country, the next big hurdle was none other than the American Embassy. Tony called them and explained that TWA airlines was ceasing services to Moscow the very next day, so if it wouldn't be too much trouble, they'd like their interview with the U.S. consular and the ensuing visa that afternoon. Well, that was not to be. In fact, the embassy informed them rather unemotionally that it would most certainly be weeks before the interview could be granted.

They had Masha, that was true, and with thankful hearts they realized that maybe a few more days in Moscow would be good for her transition, as Masha spoke nothing but Russian and had already had one traumatic transition that she'd had to endure as she left the orphanage. Maybe a few days would be all right.

However, after looking at reality as well as their diminishing finances, it was decided that perhaps Tony had better take the flight out on the last plane and at least save them having to buy him a new ticket as well, so it was settled that he would leave the next morning on that last TWA plane.

34

There was to be a big farewell dinner that night, celebrating Masha's successful adoption and travel papers. Of course, that meant food: lots of it. In fact, it was undoubtedly more food than little Masha had ever seen in one place. There was borscht, the cabbage and beetroot soup which was a mainstay in Russia. There were sausages, bought only because the host had a military veteran ration card which allowed him to buy meat. Add to that crusty bread rolls and of course, a cake.

But first, there had to be a bath, and it was soon discovered that Masha had never had a real bath before. In the orphanage, they had evidently just simply scrubbed the children off, using a bucket and brush; effective but lacking in the usual bath time frivolities. At first, the prospect of being placed in three inches of standing water had terrified her. But then she grew accustomed to it, and even allowed the water level to be increased in small increments. Finally, she found the experience positively enjoyable, and wouldn't have come out of the tub willingly had there not been the promise of food.

The party commenced, with toasts and congratulations to all. Masha ran screaming around the table in delight, a piece of food in each hand. Lots of 'aunties' and 'uncles' cheered her on, being captured by her happiness.

However, as they were having the last coffee, the phone rang. It was Vitali, the driver, or actually a friend of Vitali who was speaking for him as an interpreter.

"Where was the rest of his money?" he asked.

"I don't know what you mean," said Tony. "We've paid you the agreed price, and even added a hundred dollars more, in appreciation for all your extra effort at the immigration office."

When this was all finally communicated and repeated a couple of times, Vitali grumbled an unhappy good bye. When Tony returned to the table and reported what had happened, everyone had several derogatory comments in Russian accompanied with the clicking of tongues and nodding of heads in disgust, but it was hard to put a damper on the party. They all hoped that Vitali would go away and leave everyone alone.

When Tony and Marsha had started out for Russia, people who seemed to know said there would be bribes at every step, but when they offered the orphanage some money, they were answered with a stern, "What? You would do that and cheapen this experience?"

Ah, but that was the country, and this was the city, so the hundred dollars "tip" to Vitali had been expected after all! (even though it must be noted here that Nadia and Alla never asked for anything else after all their hard work).

The party drew to a close, goodbyes were said to Tony, who would be leaving at 4AM, and Masha was put to bed, according to the orphanage standards of 'Bed at seven!' It had been a wonderful evening.

The next morning, after Tony had kissed his two Marshas goodbye and slipped out into the cold night, the phone rang. It was Vitali, "Your husband promised me another one thousand dollars," he said to Marsha, through the interpreter.

"I'm sure he would have mentioned that to me," insisted Marsha, wiping sleep from her eyes and wondering what time it was. "No, Vitali, we do appreciate all that you're done, but feel that we've paid all that is necessary, ...and then some."

"Very well," said Vitali, sternly, this time in his own words. "Just remember......you ... trouble... at airport, I... there!"

It didn't take a lot of imagination to hear the veiled threat in his final words. Relating the conversation to Nadia a few hours later, Nadia's reply couldn't hide her concern. "We need to move you and little Masha out of this apartment to a place that Vitali doesn't know about," she said.

After calling around, she found an acquaintance who agreed to let mother and daughter stay with her until after the interview at the American embassy, scheduled for two weeks later. This woman had a sick child and needed the "hard currency" of American dollars necessary to buy medicine. It was agreed that Marsha would be paying ten US dollars a day for room and board, and the Marshas and Nadia made their way quickly across town to the new residence. Marsha sighed with relief to be moving away from Vitali, but then remembered. "Oh, what about the airport?" asked Marsha. "If he has as much influence as he seems to have, he can just wait until we start to leave, then intercept us there."

"I'm sure you're right," frowned Nadia. "I guess you

better be prepared to pay him when you want to leave, meanwhile let's just concentrate on getting you ready to leave Russia"

In fact, the Woods family was to learn several weeks later from an American military friend that Russia had soon after their departure developed the technology to put a "red flag" on the passport of anyone they wished to harass.   From that day on, any time her passport number was presented to any immigration official, instructions were given to make life as difficult as possible for the bearer.

By God's design, however, this technology did not get put into use until after Marsha and Masha had left the country.   Furthermore, since the original tickets had been made null and void by the closing down of the airline, they had to secure a flight on a totally different airline, which was to prove to be a godsend soon.

Meanwhile, back in America, Marsha's father had starting receiving calls demanding more money. Evidently the 'friend of a friend' who had been instrumental in getting them to Russia in the first place, had become emboldened by the news of the successful adoption and was thinking that she'd like a little more for her services. "Your daughter and her husband are in grave danger," he was told. "We can help them, but it will take about $5000."

Fortunately, Marsha's father wasn't born yesterday, and had been in contact with Marsha and knew they were relatively safe. However, when the caller wouldn't let up, he began to ask some questions and soon it was revealed that she had come into the US on less than honest declarations, and was in fact an illegal alien.

The next time she called, he told her sweetly, "I really am concerned about the safety of my daughter and her husband. I'm also concerned about your visa. Why don't we try to sort out both problems? I've taken the liberty of calling my congressman, who will be in touch with you soon."

There were no more demands for money after that.

A few months later it was reported that she was back in Russia, rather ironically selling a nutritional weight loss program. Ironic, because the general public was at that time struggling to put food on the table.. Still, Tony and Marsha had to thank her for having the 'whatever' to get them started on the quest for an orphan.

Tony made it safely back to America, and to Marsha's parent's house. Together, they waited and prayed, although Tony admits that the reception was a bit frosty, since in their eyes he had left their daughter and new granddaughter basically only because of wanting to save money! Oh well, at least they couldn't accuse him of being a spendthrift. They had a relaxing two weeks and Tony had time to reconnect with son, Nathan, who'd been left behind when Mom and Dad had been in Russia. Now they hiked and saw friends, generally enjoying the Colorado Rockies, all the while praying for safety and expediency for the Marshas.

Think about it :

The experience with Vitali was a real lesson in what God can use to accomplish His purposes. Here was a man who didn't believe in God, and certainly had no interest other than making money from my parents. However, God put him in just the right place and time, and used his "special talents" to accomplish what no one else could have done.

Wait for the Lord; be strong and take heart and wait for the Lord   Psalm 27:14

Chapter Six

Waiting

During those next two weeks, mother and daughter got to know each other a little better. One day was spent at the doctor's office, checking out little Masha and confirming that, except for the Strabismus, and being underweight (10 kilos or 22 pounds), she was an exceptionally healthy child. To celebrate the good news, they took Nadia to Moscow's newly opened MacDonald's restaurant. A wait of several hours was required, since the line extended around the block, but once inside, they settled into some traditional American fare. Masha's judgment was summed up in one word, "kaka", which if the reader is knowledgeable of a number of languages, you will know what that word means. Nadia's response was less derogatory, but nevertheless surprising: "Not bad, but of course I will never be back." "Why not?" asked Marsha. "Because of the long wait to get in?"

"Oh no," Nadia insisted. "In Russia, we are used to waiting for everything. But it's far too expensive for my family."

Marsha looked over their meal and was ashamed to realize that what she had just paid for the hamburgers, fries and cokes was more than a month's wages for an average Muscovite.

"I'm so sorry, Nadia," said Marsha. "Let me do something else for you and your daughter that would be better than a "Happy Meal."

"Actually, today is my only child, Irena's sixth birthday," countered Nadia. "She has a Barbie doll, from her last birthday, and really wants to have a Ken doll so Barbie can get married!" With that challenge ahead of them, Marsha, little Masha and Nadia left Macdonalds

43

and set out to the big government department store, GUM, to buy a 'Ken'.

As they passed the Bolshoi theater, they inquired at a small kiosk as to the price of the tickets that night for the Ballet, "Giselle". Marsha stepped up to the window, offering to pay, and the seller said, "They're FIFTY dollars each!" Marsha thought that while that was a bit pricey for her budget, it was probably a fair enough price for seeing the world famous Russian Ballet, but Nadia murmured something and pulled Marsha away.

"Marsha," she said irritatedly, "I've told you to keep your mouth shut when we're buying things!" They approached the next kiosk and walked away with three TWO dollar tickets for the evening performance. They continued the search for Ken, but he was not to be found in Moscow, so they parted and agreed to meet up later for the Ballet.

When Marsha left little Masha with the host grandma and met up with Nadia later that night, Nadia was alone. "Where's Irena" she asked.

"Oh, she had a nice birthday, but she was so depressed about not getting Ken that she decided that a tragedy like 'Giselle' would be just too much for one day, so she didn't come". Marsha was stunned at the maturity and cultural astuteness of this tiny six year old. With Nadia to guide them, they made their way into the Bolshoi Theater, where they enjoyed a beautiful evening of ballet. "What a beautiful country with such incredible talent and culture, to be facing such unnecessary hardships because of communism," thought Marsha to herself. On another night, Marsha was thrilled to learn that Billy Graham was in Moscow, and insisted on taking Nadia along to an evangelistic meeting. Nadia agreed to go, but was filled with misgiving. "I've heard so many horrible stories about Christians," she said. "Do they really eat their children?"

"How can you say such a thing!" exclaimed Marsha. "You know me by now; do I look like the kind of person who would do something like that?"

"No, of course not," said Nadia. "It's just that, well, I don't know very much about this, and what little I do know is frightening."

Nadia finally did agree to go. Again they left Masha with the kindly old grandmother "Dede" and set out for the coliseum. As they neared the entrance, they were both stunned to see the huge crowd which had gathered to hear the famous American evangelist. The stadium was designed to hold 50,000 people, but on that night there were more than 80,000 packed inside. At first, they thought they would not be able to get inside, but finally found a place to slip in. Nadia was nervous, and became even more agitated during the service, maybe because of the over crowding and fire hazard, but Marsha likes to think it was the Holy Spirit talking to her heart thru Billy Graham's message.

Joni Erickson Tada was also there, and spoke about her life as a quadriplegic. She had titled her testimony, "Why?" and spoke of how she would not have chosen to live a life paralyzed from the neck down, but that God had a purpose and a plan for her life. Marsha wondered, "Why?" as well, as it hadn't even been a year since her son Trevor had died.

Then the crowd started to sing. To Marsha, it was like the sound of angels, to hear "Just As I Am" being sung in Russian. To Nadia, however, it was just too much. "I can't stay," she said at last. "Please may we go?" They made their way outside, but the sound of the hymn singing followed them for blocks. Marsha said a prayer for her new friend, and continues to pray for her to this day, hopeful that eventually the Good News of Jesus Christ will be heard in that country so bound by the years of darkness. When they got home that night, Marsha gave Nadia her own Bible, and prayed that she would be able to read it and understand it enough to know what Jesus Christ had done for her. With tears in her eyes, Nadia accepted it with a sense of wonder. And so the days dragged on. Every day several hours were spent trying to contact the embassy for an appointment date, and every day they were refused. It began to be humorous as each day a different scenario would present itself. For example, one day after finally getting through, (it usually took 8-10 tries) the off hours recording came on. As it was a few minutes before 9AM the recording said, "This is the American Embassy. If you are an American and are needing assistance, please call back during business hours." Rather ironic, Marsha thought, as the KGB was at that moment trying to find out where she was so they could extract some more money! Another day she actually got thru and explained that the KGB was trying to extort money from her, only to be told to 'stop whining.' Of course the fact that Marsha's dad had contacted the congressman only made them mad and the feeling began to be that she just better smile and wait patiently, because they really could make her life miserable if they wanted to, even cancelling the appointment she had managed to make for two weeks later.

Think about it:

I guess we'll always wonder if Nadia and her family ever read Mom's Bible and came to know the truth about God. Sometimes all we can do is "plant the seed" and move on, trusting God for the harvest. Who can you tell God's truth to today, even if you may never know how that person will respond?

I waited patiently for the Lord; He turned to me and heard my cry.   Psalm 40:1

Chapter Seven

Finally!

ℱinally the day came. It was Monday, the 26th of October, and the appointment was for 1:30. When Marsha was the first one to arrive at the office at least 30 minutes early, she was alarmed as she began to see filing in behind her, about 50 people, carrying and pulling a various assortment of orphans. Gradually she began to realize that they were all obviously there for the "1:30" appointment as well!. She kept her cool, and when finally at 2:00, the official lunch hour was over and the shutters went up on the windows, the consular called out over the crowd, "Who's first?"

Marsha jumped up and called out "We are!" and grabbed Masha by the hand. At just that moment, Masha was busy playing with some blocks and didn't want to be disturbed, so she said, "Nyet" and threw her body limp towards the floor. Suddenly she screamed in pain and dropped her arm by her side. Marsha scooped her up and proceeded to the window, all the while Masha was screaming in pain.

The consular said, "Next! This baby is crying too much!" to which Marsha glared back, patting Masha on the back, and said, "We've waited more than two weeks for this interview and I can assure you, the baby is FINE!".

Possibly a bit cowed, the consular handed Masha a lolly-pop thru the bullet proof glass and opened her file. Masha settled down and happily licked the lolly-pop, tangling it a bit in Marsha's hair as she did. Fortunately the consular didn't notice that she was only using her right arm, leaving the left one dangling pitifully.

Within 10 minutes the much awaited interview was

over, and Marsha, Masha and Nadia left the embassy for the last time, with a lot less cash, but holding a brand new visa to the USA!

However, the problem of the arm puzzled them, as Masha wouldn't let them even approach her on that side showing she was in obvious pain. It was decided to drop into a neighborhood doctor for advice, and soon they were told, "Her arm is badly broken; go get your bandages from home and head for the city hospital!"

The look of wonder in Nadia's eyes said it all, "What kind of mother are you that you could break your daughter's arm just like that?" They went back to the apartment and asked for some tea towels to use as bandages and set off for the hospital, all the while little Masha whining weakly.

As they began the trip through town in the taxi, Marsha spoke up. "Nadia, I don't know how to say this, but I just can't let Masha have an injection." She had noticed when they'd been to the clinic for Masha's physical, that Russians were encouraged to buy their own needles if they wanted to have clean ones. By now all of those shops would be closed so they would be at the mercy of the hospital. Nadia thought for a moment and then nodded in agreement, although the idea of setting a broken arm without any injections was not pleasant.

When at length the taxi stopped in front of a wrecking yard, Marsha was a bit confused, but Nadia pointed to a narrow path that led thru to a gloomy institutional looking compound, hidden behind a tall brick wall. This was obviously the large city hospital.

By now it was dark, and very cold, as they started picking their way thru the debris. All the obvious doors were locked up tight, but finally they saw a light on in a doorway above a fire escape, about three stories up. It was wet and icy, but they decided that was their only hope, and they started up. Marsha was carrying Masha, and near the top step, she tripped on the front of her coat (again!) and the two stumbled and nearly fell. It should have been a frantic and frustrating experience, but somehow the tensions of the day just welled up and the two women began to laugh hysterically! Nadia, taking Masha, scolded her jokingly,

"Don't you hurt yourself too, I can't take care of BOTH of you!"

Thankfully, the door at the top of the fire escape swung open and within minutes Masha was being seen by a smiling young doctor. He had a large kerchief wrapped around his head (denoting that he was a doctor) and Masha thought he looked like a clown. He was bantering back and forth with her, holding her arm in his hand, and then "pop" it was over and everyone was smiling, including Masha. He then went on and explained to the two obviously uninformed women that there is a condition called 'nursemaid's elbow" and that it is a simple dislocation, but nevertheless, he chided, a child under five, because of their weaker connective tendons, should never be pulled by the arm!

With the American visa in hand and Masha's arm OK, the next day they hurried to the TWA office to see if there was indeed any way to use the defunct ticket, only to find it locked up tight. There was a note on the door saying that all ticket holding passengers would have to work it out with Delta in the future. Fortunately, the Delta ticket office was in the same building and within a couple of hours a flight was arranged for the next day, connecting back to TWA and the original ticket in Frankfurt.

So the last hurdle was only to make it to the airport

and fly out. Marsha tucked the thousand dollars she expected to be giving Vitali in order to get out of the country in her money belt and finished packing. There was a tearful goodbye to Nadia and Alla and the next morning they left in the early dawn.

On the way to the airport, Marsha began to realize that this airport was not the same one into which she and Tony had arrived almost a month before. As she looked about nervously, the taxi driver sensed her confusion and said confidently, "Delta!" Obviously, this airport was another one of five Moscow airports and it was used by Delta, but NOT by TWA. Through God's ingenuity and the loss of their tickets, whatever noose Vitali had prepared for them had been successfully slipped.

Think about it:

I know Mom has always felt bad about dislocating my arm, but when you think about it, all she did was hold me. I was the one who pulled away with a "nyet!" How often do we hurt ourselves by simply pulling away from the way God has set out for us? His way is always best, and refusing to go that way can only bring us pain and misery. Believe me, I know!

but those who hope in the Lord will renew their strength.
They will soar on wings like eagles   Isaiah 40:31

Chapter Eight

Flight

They boarded the plane without incident, much to Marsha's relief, but of course, as this was Marsha's first flight with Masha, tensions were high.

As they settled down in their seats for the flight, Masha clutched to her chest the most precious gift from Nadia, six beautiful apples (called yablushka). As soon as the seatbelt was secured, she started eating. She was sitting between her new Mom and a NASA scientist who took some interest in her and her apples, trying to talk to her and otherwise entertain her, even offering his calculator to her to distract her. Wrong. Nothing would distract her from her precious yablushkas. It had evidently been a reward in the orphanage to be given a shriveled piece of apple if you had to visit the infirmary, so this was a real big haul, to have six!

She munched thru one after the other, relishing each bite of apple, peeling, seeds and stem. Marsha thought bemusedly that in Japan children are alarmed to even find a piece of skin on their carefully cut and sliced apples, but here sat this little girl, obviously in heaven with her treasure. Finally, as Masha began to help herself to apple number four, Marsha looked at the scientist, and they both nodded, "enough". Here was a child who weighed barely 10 kilos (22 lbs) and surely four apples were enough. Wrong again. The screaming and the grabbing began. Off came the seatbelt and it was like having a visit from the Tasmanian Devil, this precious child who'd learned somewhere how to guard what was hers!

By then the plane was landing in Frankfurt and Masha was screaming at the top of her lungs, "DIE DIE DIE!" What a funny coincidence that the word for "give me" in Russian means something completely different in English and isn't really something you're wanting to hear screamed out as your on final approach to landing in an airplane!

As soon as they got off the plane, Marsha put Masha in her newly acquired stroller and ran for the gate, hoping to make their connection back onto a TWA plane. However, as soon as they identified themselves, the agent said curtly, "Sorry Ma'am , the gate is closed, you'll have to spend the night in Frankfurt" After the flight they'd just been on, that was definitely the last thing she wanted to hear.

She begged the agent, "Please, please let me just run onto the plane, I really can't go into an unknown city with this MONSTER child!"

The agent leaned over the counter to see Masha sleeping angelically in her stroller, exhausted from the apple incident. She gave Marsha a withering stare and Marsha slumped away from the counter and looked around for a place to sit down and ponder what she needed to do. Just as she was about to despair, she heard a booming man's voice behind her, directing his speech to the agent.

"Excuse me," he said, as he reached over the counter and tapped the service manual, "but you need to re-read your book," he said. "I realize you're trying to get her back on your TWA plane, but you'll remember that if the connecting flight is impossible to make through no fault of the passenger, you are REQUIRED keep her on her original airline"

The agent looked cowed and began to fill out paperwork issuing yet another ticket on Delta. Marsha turned to look in disbelief at this stranger who was smiling at her and extending his hand.

"Hello, I'm a Delta pilot who was riding dead head on the plane you were on. I could tell from the screaming that you were adopting an orphan, you see, I've done the same thing twice!"

What a happy meeting that was, and as they sat down to wait for the next plane, he shared some stories of his adventures in Russia.

"By the way," he said, "You'll have to turn that US visa over in New York when you arrive and it'll take you six weeks to get it back. That'll keep you from getting her citizenship or any other immigration status until you get it back. Would you like me to step back into the

58

Delta offices and see if I can get it copied for you?"

"Of course!" she shouted, relieved that this 'angel' had happened by. But as he strode away with the visa she caught herself and said, "You realize it's taken me a month to get that visa and I don't know you at all......."

He turned laughing and said, "You have my bag!".
True to his word, he was back in just a minute with a copy that would be able to be used immediately to begin the immigration process in America. From there, it was on to New York, then finally to Denver, Colorado, where Dad, brother Nathan, Grandma and Grandpa were waiting to meet this much awaited little girl.

Think about it:

Back in Russia, God used an athiest to accomplish His will in our lives. Then later at the Frankfurt airport, He used a fellow believer. It seems that there's no limit to who, and what God can use to make sure things go according to His plan. Are you worried that the people and places around you will keep God from making you all you were created to be? Think again.

for He satisfies the thirsty and fills the hungry with good things   Psalm 107:9

Chapter Nine

America, Land of Friends and Food

*M*asha recalls: When I got off the plane, I was so surprised to see my new brother, Nathan, holding a big stuffed dog. It was kind of scary, but he was smiling, so I thought it might be all right. I had a big Russian bow in my hair, actually tied in this time, and a new dress, and even though I'd been on the plane almost 24 hours, I was very excited! We went up into the mountains where my new Grandma and Grandpa lived, and finally settled in a real bed for a few hours of real sleep.

The next few days were a celebration as the new Woods family shopped and caught up with old friends. By now, all Russian speakers had been left far behind, much to Masha's frustration. Often, she would say something, only to be met with a smile and a pat on the head. When that happened, she would say it louder, sometimes accompanied by a vigorous stomp of the foot. But there was no communicating with the poor girl, except for the dozen or so words her new parents had picked up in Russia. Amidst all the gibberish, she was relieved from time to time to hear "morodietz" (good girl), or "spasiba" (thank you).

She still had quite a problem with food. In the orphanage there had evidently never been enough, because Masha faced real trauma when the food would be cleared away. In America, there is always plenty to eat, but even though it's everywhere, there still remain somewhat defined meal times and Masha would cry and cry when the meal was over and she couldn't gorge on anymore food. Finally Marsha's Dad, who was for the most part rather austere when it came to childhood behavior, had this to offer:

"Let her hold a bread roll when we clear the table".

With that assurance of unending food, the dramas stopped immediately.

On the first Sunday in Colorado, a baby dedication was planned, to be held at Evergreen Baptist, Tony and Marsha's home church. Everyone was a little nervous, wondering how little Masha would react to all the attention. They needn't have worried, though, since as soon as they stepped up to the front of the church, Masha, who was being held by Marsha, first smiled and waved at everyone and then discovered her Mom's bra, and kept trying to reach it, shouting out "Maika! Maika!" (undershirt) at the top of her lungs. Fortunately only the parents had any idea what she was saying and the dedication proceeded without a hitch. The whole church family prayed together: prayers of gratitude for this gift from God, and prayers for protection and blessing for years to come, as this tiny Russian child became an American missionary kid who would be growing up in Japan.

Before that could happen, though, little Masha would need a Japanese visa, and this proved almost the undoing of the whole effort.

Think about it:

Even though I was quite young, I can still remember the frustration and fear of being in a new environment where my words carry no meaning to the people around me. Stomping my foot didn't help, and it wasn't until I began to learn the new words that peace finally came. Every day, we get placed in circumstances where people around us can't seem to hear what we're saying, and this is especially true when you're trying to communicate spiritual truth. Maybe the key for those times is the same thing that helped me: try to learn what the people around you are saying in their hearts, then speak that language to them. God's truth doesn't have to be a big mystery; it just needs to be spoken in a way people can understand.

but our citizenship in is Heaven   Philippians 3:20

Chapter Ten

Hawaii

$\mathcal{T}$ony and Marsha had heard that US immigrations and visas were the easiest to get in Hawaii, so they left Colorado, on their way back home to Japan, planning to stop for a few days in Honolulu, to get either a US passport and visa or at least a Japanese visa in her Russian passport and head on for home.

When the plane landed, they were met by the Gierhart family, fellow missionaries to Japan who were on Stateside assignment at the time. They festooned everyone with Hawaiian Leis, which greatly excited Masha, as

64

hers was made of candy.

Immediately after leaving the airport, they drove to the Bureau of Immigration and Naturalization to see if Masha could become an American citizen right away, but were told it would take at least six months. "That's no good" they thought, so they headed for the Japanese consulate.

At first the Japanese were nice, until they realized they were not dealing with an American. "This child has a Russian passport," the official said.

"Yes, we just adopted her," said Marsha. "Is that a problem?"

"She is a Communist" she replied flatly . "Japan does not want Communists."

"She's three years old!" exclaimed Tony, rather incredulously, "I can assure you she is no Communist."

"Nevertheless," the official said, turning away, "come back tomorrow."

Hearing that, Tony and Marsha felt a shudder of dread.

After 14 years living and working in Japan, they knew that the Japanese people, while extremely gracious, were not particularly confrontational. Rather than say "no" to a particular request, they would simply smile and nod, or else re-schedule the meeting... again ... and again, until the other party finally gave up. Their fears were confirmed over the next several days, as time and again, they went to the consulate, only to be told, "Come back later.......... maybe tomorrow."

It looked like it was going to be a long haul, so they asked their good friends, Bob and Gail Gierhart, if they could stay with them for awhile until the problem was sorted out. The Gierharts were old friends and were more than willing to take the Woods into their home. So began the wait. After a week of everyday visits to the consulate, it was decided once again that Tony and Nathan should precede Marsha and Masha back to Japan in order to get back to work and school. They were sure that the visa would come through any day.

Now Marsha and little Masha began to settle into a routine of being somewhat unplanned for houseguests. Of course the Gierharts were more than gracious, being a very generous and loving family, but it was a crowded existence to be sure. The Gierhart children, who were

66

10, 7 and 5, had all been moved into one room, and if that wasn't bad enough, they also soon discovered that this little terror of a Russian could hear bath water running from anywhere in the house and would run stripping her clothes off to join them, invited or not! If they closed the door, she banged and screamed until they gave in and let her join them. She still spoke no English and assumed that everyone could understand her perfectly, choosing to rattle on incessantly, no matter if they were trying to have their own conversation or watch a TV program. She considered sleep a weakness, so there were many battles at bedtime, but she always awoke bright and early, ready to start a new day of discovery, even when that included waking up all her new found friends. Marsha worried about her indefatigable curiosity and was concerned that the only word she would learn would be "no!".

Masha recalls:
So many new changes! One change I remember was the car seat. It was fun to ride in cars in Russia where you could roam at will, but in the USA, car seats are mandatory, and because I still only weighed 10 kilos, I definitely needed to be confined. This was not a happy time, because my Mom wouldn't give in to my wishes, but gradually I resigned myself to being strapped in be-

fore the the car would move. I think the poor Gierhart family had to endure a lot of screaming!.

One particular day, as they were riding toward home after church, Bob said to Gail, in an interlude between screams, "Do you think we should stop and eat?" As Masha caught her breath for yet another blast, there was sudden silence as her eyes got big. From her seat came her first English word, spoken so quietly as to almost go unnoticed and then louder and louder.........
..."EAT?" Her soon-to-become beloved "Uncle Bob" had hit on what was her most motivating goal, to eat! She used her new word often and began to add words daily.

This was also the period of time when Aunt Gail began to use her middle name Nicole. It had always been the plan to call her by Nicki, or Nicole, but at first they had kept the name 'Masha' just to avoid putting any more confusion on the poor child. However, as the time in Hawaii dragged on, the name 'Nicki' began to be more and more comfortable for everyone, even Nicki!

Because Marsha had no car and a limited budget, the days evolved into riding to the nearest beach or shopping center with the Gierharts as they left for the day,

68

and then just milling around or sitting at the beach till being picked up again. Mother and daughter got to know each other, but both were probably wondering just what they'd embarked upon. Of course, every day focused around calling or visiting in person the Japanese consulate, only to be told "not today".

Finally Marsha could stand it no more and started by getting quite stern with the Japanese consulate. "Look here" she said in Japanese so there'd be no mistake, "I saw a sign in the Moscow Japanese embassy that said Russians had to wait for 30 days before getting a visa, and it's been more than 30 days, so I WANT my visa!"

After a few moments of silence, the secretary shifted in her seat and answered enigmatically, avoiding Marsha's stare, "Oh, it may be several more months yet."

Marsha stormed out of the consulate and headed down the street to the American Immigration and Naturalization office dragging Nicki by the arm she had been cautioned not to pull. Even though they had been told on the first day it would take at least six months for Nicki to become a citizen, Marsha thought she just HAD to ask again.

At the reception desk she was preparing to state her case, but instead just broke down and cried. The old saying that a woman's tears will work wonders certainly was true and she was quickly ushered into a side room. Perhaps the idea was to get her out of the waiting room quickly lest others lose heart as well, but it worked. As soon as she explained that she just didn't think she had what it took to wait in Hawaii for another five or six months, they seemed quite surprised.

They asked, "Are both you and your husband American citizens?....... yes?......Well if that's the case, it only takes a day to make her a naturalized US citizen! Whoever told you differently?" they exclaimed as they rolled their eyes at each other and nodded to the back office knowingly.

Within two days, with a shining new American passport, duly stamped with a Japanese visa in hand, they set off for Japan. What a relief to be finally heading home. It had been almost three months since meeting Masha in Russia to landing in Japan with her as an American citizen with a new name, Nicki!.

Once again, she was scrubbed up and dressed up in her best outfit, and by now had begun to speak enough

English to get by fairly well (at least for a three year old). The big bow was tied securely in her hair, and she could sense that something exciting was about to happen. Coming out of Japanese customs at Tokyo's Narita Airport, she was delighted to see her new Dad again, and there was her new brother! It was such a happy time, and Marsha cried for joy and relief that the 'adventure' was finally over.

A crowd of Japanese friends and church members had also gathered to greet them, some of them driving for hours to be there. As they exchanged greetings and caught up on the news, Marsha began to be aware of two tiny eyes boring in on her. Looking at Nicki, she saw in her face a look of confusion, with just a hint of real anger. Then she realized: everyone was speaking Japanese! After three months of hearing, becoming accustomed to, and even learning to speak English, now the rules had been changed. Nicki was not happy, and she let everyone know.

"I'm sorry, Sweetie," Marsha said, giving her daughter a big hug. Don't worry: you'll be speaking this new language before you know it!"

And so she would.

Think about it:

I still think it's funny that the Japanese embassy classified me as a "Communist", even though I was only three years old. So many times, it seems, we get put into boxes that don't define us. What really counts is not the outside tags and handles, but what lies at the heart. Who are you, really?

God sets the lonely in families   Psalm 68:6

Chapter Eleven

Japan, My New Home

ℒife in Japan was a real challenge for me at first. Russian was still my first language, although I had begun picking up a little English. And boy, did I have plenty to talk about! This was a whole new world for me, with none of the people and places which had been an every day part of my first three years of life. Each day, I would babble on incessantly about this, that or the other. At least it sounded like "babbling" to everyone around me, much to my anger and frustration. I mean, c'mon guys, I'm baring my soul here, only to have them smile and pat me on the head and say things like "kawaii neh!" (Isn't she cute?). And that brings up the other challenge, which was to learn not one, but TWO new languages simultaneously. If looks could kill that day at Narita Airport, my new Mom would have been in real trouble. For over a month, we'd been struggling to communicate with each other, mostly through smiles and food, and I had been making real progress (especially with the food motivation). Now all of a sudden, I found myself in a world where neither Russian nor my limited English had any effect on anyone, except to make them come back with sounds I'd never heard before. Thank goodness my parents and brother at least still spoke English to me.

I must have expressed my frustration. My poor parents knew I was grieving over leaving the orphanage, but they didn't know how to help. Then one day my dad decided to take me with him to the church 'yochien' (which is Japanese for preschool). Every week he took his guitar and sang songs in English and Japanese with the kids. They loved it, and they loved him. Dad said the place reminded him a lot of the orphanage where I came from, except that the kids all went home to families every day. Usually I stayed home while he went about his work, but this day for some reason Dad took

74

me along. The first minute I saw the place, I knew this was where I belonged. Here was a whole room full of people just my size! There were teachers and little chairs and … food! One of the teachers took my hand while Dad went to the front of the room with his guitar. He started to sing, and soon all the kids were singing too, at the top of their lungs. I didn't understand the Japanese words they were singing, but I could see that they were happy and having a good time. Letting go of the teacher's hand, I proceeded right to the front of the group, found an empty chair and sat down. From that moment on, everyone knew that I was going to be okay. After the songs, kids got up to play. I don't remember exactly what they were doing, but I do remember every child in the room coming up to me. They wanted to see this "gaijin" (Japanese for "foreigner") and shake my hand. I started to be scared of all the attention, but a smile from my Dad told me that it was okay. Before the end of the day I was jumping and running with all the kids, and soon after I began to bring Japanese words home.

I'll always be grateful to that yochien. It was in a small town called Yoshioka. Dad would just have to say the word, "Yoshioka?" and I'd be putting my shoes on and heading out the door. Through getting to know the children and teachers there, I was starting to know more about this new world I'd been brought to.

I may have had some doubts about it at first, but now I was beginning to see that it was okay after all. God blessed me in very many ways those first few weeks, but Yoshioka was probably the biggest blessing of all.

Think about it:

What was it about Yoshioka yochien that did so much for my adjustment? Was it the kids, who reminded me of my orphanage roots? Was it the music that Dad sang? I sang along too, with great enthusiasm, even though at first I didn't have a clue what I was singing. Maybe that was it: the enthusiasm I felt, from my Dad, from the children and the teachers. I knew neither the words nor the meanings of the songs they sang, but they were so excited about them that I knew it must be something good. Why can't we live the same way as Christians? People may not know at first what we're going on about, but if we say it with enthusiasm, they're going to want to know more!

Open my eyes that I may see wonderful things ...

Psalm 119:18

Chapter Twelve

New Eyes

$\mathcal{B}$ut now that I was safe and sound in my new home, Mom and Dad set about to get my eyes fixed. They took me to the local eye doctor there where we lived in Japan. It was just a small northern town, but were they ever surprised to find that one of the world's best eye doctors had a clinic there! For many years he had worked in a famous research hospital in America, and now he was back in his home town, doing what he did best: fixing crossed eyes.

The process was not exactly an easy one, at least for a three year old who spoke no Japanese. For months, I had routine appointments where they assessed my vision using puppets and having me point to where they were. They were really talented in working with small children. Before I was three and a half, we had a surgery date set. Of course, I had to go and catch a cold, so the surgery was postponed. This happened two or three times, because I was having to 'get to know' all the new germs and viruses that I had never come across in my isolation at the orphanage in Russia, so I had the sniffles most of the first year in Japan.

At any rate, the day finally came when I was well enough to be operated on. I had to be admitted to the hospital overnight before the surgery and for two nights after the surgery. In Japan when children have to stay in the hospital, a family member is expected to stay with the child. They even have a special word for it: "tsukisoi", which means 'attached carer'. Mom always laughed because it sounded an awful lot like another Japanese word, "chikisho", which is something you should never say!

The surgery seemed to me to last a long time, but they said it was routine. Afterwards I was pretty drugged
78

and miserable, trying to scratch at my painful eyes and not understanding what anyone was saying to me. But thanks to the skill of my new doctor friend, the surgery was a complete success and I now had a new pair of eyes. I look at pictures of myself before the surgery, and even though everyone says I was cute with crossed eyes, I'm still grateful that it could be corrected. I still wear glasses to correct my vision, but, like most everyone I know, I have a pair of contacts which I can pop in anytime when I want to do sports or just 'glam' up. Besides, like my Mom told me, "There are two kinds of people in the world: people who wear glasses, and people who don't wear glasses YET!"

I'm so happy that God gave me crossed eyes, so that I could be adopted. Then God also provided a great doctor in a small town who was able to fix them, and loving parents who had the courage to keep going and get it taken care of.

In yochien, one of my favorite songs was "Kagayake, Shu no eiko, chi no ue ni". ("Shine Jesus shine.") Maybe even then I could see what Jesus was doing in my life, taking me out of a dark situation with no future, placing me in a home where Jesus' light shone strong, and fixing my eyes so I could see all He had done.

Those first few years of my life there in Japan were real eye openers, in a lot of ways! They helped make me what I am now, and I'll always be grateful. I thank God now for the chance to shine for Him.

One of the first people to model that kind of living in the light was the girl who would become my very best friend, Yuu Ito. Our parents worked together at the church and although she was several years older than me, she quickly assumed the role of big sister in my life. She played with me, took care of me, and taught me about Japan, and about life. She helped me grow spiritually and emotionally, and modeled the kinds of life goals that could only come true if we believed in Jesus Christ and believed in ourselves to achieve them. The goal in my life at this time was just to live and love Christ. It was harder than I thought it would be but my loving parents and Yuu helped me get through these times.

Think about it:

I have to be honest: eye surgery was not fun, especially for a kid like I was, placed in a world where nothing was like anything I remembered from the orphanage. I've said in this chapter that I'm grateful for having crossed eyes, but I have to admit that there are times when I wonder why God couldn't have just worked another miracle and brought me to this place without all the trauma. But then, I think, sometimes pain and trauma accomplish things in a person's life that just can't be done any other way. It's the world we live in, and it makes the promise of the world to come so much the better.

...you are no longer foreigners and aliens, but fellow citizens with God's people...   Ephesians 2:19

Chapter Thirteen

Eating Pigeons

*a*s I was soon to learn, fitting into new situations was just part and parcel for life as a missionary kid. Most of our time was spent in Japan, but during the first four years in my new home, we also spent time in Hong Kong, America and Ethiopia

After two years of yochien, I was ready at last for the first grade, and I have to say it got easier and easier as

I did it about five times! What? That's right, I went to the first grade five times. Oh, but I only finished once!

It all started when Mom and Dad told me that we were going to go live in Hong Kong for a month and then go to Ethiopia for three months. My Dad was asked first of all to be an interim pastor for a Japanese congregation in Hong Kong for a month, then also at the same time was given a chance to teach the Bible to Sudanese refugees in a camp in southwest Ethiopia near a place called Gambela.

He and Mom talked about it, and decided it would be a good experience for everybody. As we were getting ready to go to America for a short home assignment anyway, this would only be a couple of stopovers, long enough to give us kids a chance to see some other aspects of missionary work.

I wasn't old enough to have much opinion about it yet, but my brother Nathan expressed enough for both of us. He was fifteen at the time, and at the peak of his "teenage years". Hong Kong sounded okay to him, mainly because of all the shopping opportunities, but Ethiopia was a different story. What was he supposed to do, 500 miles from the nearest phone or television for three months? Mom and Dad explained to him that finding the answer to that question was one of the main reasons we were going in the first place, but it was hard for him to accept.

As it turned out though, he had a wonderful experience in both Hong Kong and Ethiopia, and in a lot of ways that's where his call to ministry came to him. He's even been back to Hong Kong on a couple of short term mission assignments, and to Africa twice. I'm pretty proud of him.

We arrived in Hong Kong the day I had graduated from yochien. You can imagine how tired I was! We had the big graduation and ensuing party, said goodbye to everyone for a year, ran for the Shinkansen (bullet train) that would take us to Tokyo, transferred to the airport and right on to the four hour flight to Hong Kong. We were met at the airport by my Dad (who had been in New Zealand doing a Japanese wedding) and some new Japanese friends.

I still remember them taking us out for Chinese food. It was funny, because the main course was pigeon! It struck us all as funny, because just as we were leaving our home in Japan, I had put out the last bit of bird̲ ̲ed for our family of pigeons that we called "Mr. and Mrs. Rufus", and now we were dining on their relatives! My brother and I understood the withering looks from my parents, though, and didn't voice any objections to the meal. Hong Kong was certainly going to be an interesting place, I figured!

Our apartment was on the fourth floor of a 24 story building. There were about twenty identical looking buildings all sitting together in an area of Hong Kong called Tai Koo Shin. Because the entrances were identical, you had to know where you lived by the surroundings. We were right after the fruit shop on the right, next to the bank. If I just stood on my tippy toes, I could reach our call button to type in the code for the lock on the door. If it opened, then we knew we were at the right place.

Within a few days I was enrolled in the first grade at Hong Kong Japanese school. My parents figured at that stage in my life, my best language was Japanese, although most people said I spoke "champon", which is a word for casserole. They'd say, "You know, your language is all mixed together like a casserole!"

But besides that, I'd become used to having Japanese teachers and classmates, and everyone thought I'd have less adjustment problems by going into first grade alongside Japanese boys and girls who had just finished yochien like I had. Also, they knew I'd be back in Japan within the year, so I might as well stick with one educational system, even if it was only for a month.

How exciting it was to have my first "Nugakkyshiki" (entrance ceremony) with my new uniform, backpack and all. It was very formal and I was a little bit scared, but I soon made friends. We rode the special bus every morning and afternoon from Tai Koo Shin all the way up the hill on Hong Kong Island to the Japanese school. It was always fun, and after school, my parents and brother would explore all over the city, visiting church members or going with them to places they wanted to show us. It was a month we'll never forget, and we still keep in touch with the people there.

Think about it:

After moving through Russian, English and Japanese environments, finding myself thrust into a Chinese speaking world was not so big of a shock, especially since school and home were still places I could communicate. It did open my eyes a little wider, though, to the fact that the world is full of lots of different kinds of people who think of their own hometowns as "normal". Who am I to think that my own background is the only one that counts, in God's eyes? Lord, help me see the world from Your point of view, and help me to love the wolrd as You do.

...to shine on those living in darkness and in the shadow of death, to guide our feet into the path of peace.

Luke 1:79

Chapter fourteen

Air Hyena

*B*efore we knew it, we were saying good bye to all of our new friends and heading for Ethiopia. First stop was Addis Ababa, where we were met by old friends of my parents who were serving as missionaries there.

We hadn't been there more than 24 hours before we were ALL FOUR so sick we thought we would die! At first we thought it was something we had eaten, but then the next door neighbor came down with the same fever. The doctor said it just seemed to be a case of breathing in at the wrong time. Africa still has lots of unknown diseases, and they're especially hard on newcomers. I've read since then that back in the 1800s, the average LIFE EXPECTANCY of a missionary in Africa was four months! Our poor friends really had to put up with a lot during that first week. Fortunately the Mom was a nurse, and she made five beds (her daughter was sick too) on the living room floor, and tried to keep us full of fluids and medicine. There was only one bathroom in the house and we kept it busy.

What an introduction for my brother and me to Africa. For the most part, all I can remember is sleeping a lot, waking up to worried expressions from people I didn't know, then drifting off again. My Dad says that's all he remembers as well.

It took about a week before we had recovered enough to think about traveling on out to the refugee camp where we were supposed to live for the next three months. We were to fly there on a small plane the missionaries laughingly called the "vomit comet", not a word we particularly wanted to hear just then!

My dad laughingly tells the story of going up to the desk at the airport and asking when the 8:30AM plane would actually be leaving. The reply was "ahhh....... Maybe 2:00". Usually my dad was pretty calm, but he was incredulous at the answer, and raising his voice just a bit exclaimed, "2:00???"

The chagrined agent replied, "OK how about 1:30?"

We made it to the camp safe and sound, although the pilot spent a lot of time circling, trying to see through the clouds. They didn't have much in the way of navigation systems out there, so they depended on things like rivers, villages and mountain ranges to know where they were going.

Touching down on the grass runway near Gambela, our hearts were all in our throats. We had started our experience early that day finding out that the plane would be leaving many, many hours late for no apparent reason. I don't remember when we actually left, but we were very, very late arriving. As the refugee camp missionaries only checked messages once a day by radio, there was no way to tell them that we would be late, so naturally they had given up on us arriving that day.

It was about 5 PM by now, and when we landed, the other five passengers responded by clapping and cheering. I wondered to myself if the landing was an unusual happening. The airport was the most interesting one I'd ever seen. It consisted of a bit of smooth grass and one tree with a wire hanging on it. My Mom was desperate for a bathroom and was eyeing the tree, checking to see if it was big enough to hide behind, when a Land Rover careened up and a lady jumped out and started chasing after the retreating plane that had just dropped us off! I've heard of 'running for your flight', but I've never heard of chasing down the plane! Sure enough, the plane turned around and picked her up. We later found out that she was a UN doctor who had abandoned hope of flying out that day until she heard the plane overhead and had raced for the airport. As the other passengers piled into the UN Land Rover with all their bags, the driver indicated to us that we should load up as well so we could ride the 30 miles into Gambella village and find a place to stay. He knew who we were and knew the missionaries would come back into town the next day to get us.

Being Westerners, and even having a Japanese mindset of not wanting to bother anyone, we said politely, "Oh, No thank you; we'll just wait here."

The UN man threw his head back, laughed jovially and said, "When it gets dark, the only thing coming to meet you will be the hyenas!"

With that vivid imagery in our minds, we couldn't get into the already overcrowded Land Rover fast enough! I was thrown into the back on top of the luggage and my Mom was the fourth passenger in the front seat, straddling the gear shift. Bumping into Gambella way after dark, we went to the only place that seemed to have lights. It was a combination restaurant, bar, grocery store, post office, and to our great delight, motel. The rooms we were given were made of cement blocks and each contained a single bed, mosquito net and plenty of rats, but we were just thankful to be on the ground and relatively safe. When I saw the one communal toilet, I decided I might want to wait to use it for another day!

Think about it:

For us, Ethiopia was a great adventure, but I really have to admire those early missionaries for whom Africa was their grave. Unlike missionaries today, those brave men and women didn't have telephones, email, furloughs and modern transportation. They simply heard the call of God and they went. Where would you be willing to go, if God called you? What kinds of things would make you say, "Oh no, Lord, not there!" Those are the things you need to pray about, because they're walls between you and God. And no one wants walls.

The boundary lines have fallen for me in pleasant places...   Psalm 16: 6

Chapter Fifteen

Settling In

Sure enough, the next morning, the missionaries met us, thinking we would be arriving that day. What a happy reunion with people we'd never met! Food and supplies were loaded into their truck, and we set off for Bonga, the site of the refugee camp. There were over a thousand people there, mostly of the Uduk tribe, and we were amazed to learn that almost all of them were Christians. In fact, that was why they were refugees, having been persecuted by the Islamic forces back in

Sudan. About a year earlier, the whole tribe decided to leave Sudan, choosing to walk to safety. On the three month exodus, nearly half of them died on the way to Ethiopia, either from Sudanese rebels, disease or starvation. Coming over the Ethiopian border, the United Nations arranged for them to be allowed to stay, provided they never left the isolated area where they were, at least not until they could be processed and evacuated to safer places.

My dad got to work right away teaching the Old Testament to the Christian leaders of the camp. Most of them didn't read or write, and even if they could, the Old Testament had not been translated into Uduk, so they were pretty much unfamiliar with all the Old Testament stories. Dad was very impressed, however, to learn that even though they were mostly illiterate, they never forgot anything they heard!

Over the next three months, Dad took them through the Old Testament, book by book. Then at the end of the time, he asked them to tell him what they had learned. He was stunned to hear that they remembered perfectly every word he had said, even applying the stories to what they already knew in the New Testament.

Mom, Dad and I got a big mud-walled hut to sleep in, complete with a grass roof. It was a lot of fun, and since there was no bed for me, I got to sleep on top of an old steamer trunk which I called my "treasure chest". Of course we had to sleep under mosquito nets because of the threat of malaria, but nobody minded because the rats were horrible and nobody wanted them in their bed!

My brother Nathan had a grass hut all to himself, which seemed pretty nice at first, until all the rats came in to visit. He was pretty miserable for a few days, and entertained ideas of leaving on the next plane back for Addis Ababa, but God was good and sent a distraction.

We were walking around the village one morning when we discovered two brand new basketball goals laying in the dirt. When he asked about them, the kids told him that a United Nations truck had dropped them off a few weeks earlier, but no one knew what they were for.

"I know what they're for!" he yelled. Soon he had everyone out clearing a space and setting up the goals Somehow he even knew the measurements of the court and all the free throw lines, etc. By the next day, he had started basketball clinics for over 800 boys! They had no basketballs, but managed to gather up soccer balls and even some things made from woven grass. Those 'balls' didn't bounce too well, but they were good for passing and shooting practice. Needless to say, Nathan was happy from then on, and worked as hard as my parents. The village kids were thrilled to learn a new game as well.

Mom spent most of her time just providing meals for the family. There were no stores around, just a small open air market in Gambela, about an hour's drive away. She said resolutely that she wouldn't buy any meat as it was absolutely black with flies and hanging un-refrigerated out in the open. As people would make their order, the butcher would take his hand and scrape at least an inch thick 'crust' of flies from the surface before he cut some off to weigh. Just watching that almost made us sick, but fortunately there were other interesting things to buy like mealy flour or rotting vegetables so a trip to market was an exciting outing.

We had brought a lot of food with us, but we still had to make bread, find and cook what vegetables there were, and figure out how to do everything else necessary to keeping us fed. I must add that after a few weeks, we were buying the meat and just cooking it really well before we ate it! Of course with that came the need to buy a lot of limes the next time we were at the market to try to stop the diarrhea!

Fortunately, we had a lot of help from the ladies in the camp, so that made living a little easier. One woman hauled water for us from a well over two miles away. Every drop we used had to be hauled this way. Her name was Neska, and she scared me a little at first, because she was very black and looked so tough. Nathan was envious of her muscles. But what sold me was her little granddaughter, Rahab. The first time we met, Neska's face broke into a big smile and she lifted us both up in her arms and I knew I was going to have a good time in Bonga. Rahab was about my age, and we quickly became best friends. Neither of us spoke a word of the other's language, but when you're six, that doesn't matter. Rahab taught me how to grind corn on a rock (Mom said that was why she broke a tooth on a slice of bread), and I showed her how to play my American and Japanese games.

Thinking back, I can see now that Rahab was the kind of girl you see on the Africa posters: malnourished, suffering from parasites and very, very poor. But as we played together, Rahab taught me so much I'll never forget. She never complained, even when it was hot and the flies were making a nuisance of themselves crawling towards our eyes and mouth looking for water. She and her grandmother both could laugh so hard, it made me join in laughing just to hear them. She accepted her life, and helped me to understand some of the things I took for granted.

One day, Rahab's grandmother invited us to her hut for coffee. In Ethiopia, when you're invited for coffee, it means that they will take the beans that they've grown and dried, they will roast them, grind them and add the boiling water and filter it, all in the same sitting, which makes it quite an event. Ironic that the grandmother's name was "Neska" don't you think? When Neska made gestures with her broken English to invite Mom for coffee, Mom was delighted and said, "Oh, we'd love to come! What time?"

Without a second's hesitation, Rahab's grandmother just looked up to the sky, then pointed to a spot off in the west. "About there," she answered. That gave us something to do all day, watching the sun carefully until it was at about the right place before heading off for the meeting.

Rahab also taught me how to sing, Sudanese style. I didn't know the word for it then, but it's called "minor pentantic", and I think it means singing with no sharps or flats. It really sounds different than our western style of music, sort of a haunting melody. I'll never forget standing under an open sky at night, watching the stars come out and singing "Jesus Loves Me" in strange African harmonies. Rahab also taught me some Uduk songs that I still remember. Unfortunately, I don't know what the words mean, but I trust Rahab, and know they must be good words!

Rahab and her friends also braided my hair one day, and by that, I mean all day. Everyone was so amazed to touch my hair, because it was so different from theirs. I think because it was so fine that it also made braiding a lot harder, but they kept at it until it was done. I think that as a six year old, it was a big ask for me to sit still so long, but I did my best.

Think about it:

Probably the biggest miracle we experienced in Ethiopia was the one God did for my brother. At first, Nathan didn't want to go, then he didn't want to stay, even begging Mom and Dad to let him catch a UN plane back to Addis Ababa and somehow find his way back to our friend's house. But then when the basketball goals were discovered, everything changed. Suddenly, he had a purpose for being there, and it's affected his life ever since. We all need a purpose, whether it's teaching the Bible, organizing a basketball camp, or just grinding corn on a rock. And you want to know something amazing? We all DO have a purpose, given by God! What's needed is to find that purpose, and then spend the rest of our lives fulfilling it.

Teach me Your way, O Lord, and I will walk in Your truth... Psalm 86:11

Chapter Sixteen

Amazing Lessons

*E*ventually, we got used to life in Bonga. Our favorite time of day was just after sundown. The days were so hot, and we had to conserve water, so it was pretty uncomfortable. But at night we would climb up on the roof of the hut we used for cooking. It was the only metal roof in the camp, and it felt so cool.

Sometimes, young people from the camp would come up on the roof with us, to practice their English, or just to talk. One of the boys was real friendly, and he wanted to know all about the world outside of the camp. One night he asked my dad, "Have you ever seen the ocean?"

"Yes, my dad said. "It's very big."

"Once I fell in the river," the boy said. "I couldn't touch the bottom. I was so scared, I thought I would die. Is the ocean that deep?" he asked.

"Well," my dad thought out loud. "You know how far it is to the river?"

"Yes, about two miles."

"Try to imagine that distance, straight down. In places, the ocean is deeper than that."

I think from that night on, the boy didn't believe anything else my dad told him.

"Our pastor saw the ocean once," he said after awhile. "He said it was a very angry thing, always trying to get to you." He must have been talking about the waves. "But the pastor said that the ocean cannot get to you,

103

because the sand holds it back. "What a great God," he told us, "that He would choose something like the sand to hold back the ocean!"

I thought that was interesting. That pastor, and the boy who told us the story, did not know much about oceans, because they were desert people. They knew sand. Thinking about what he told us, I think to myself, sometimes I feel like a grain of sand on the beach. I'm just little, and not so much different from Rahab, or anyone else for that matter. And yet, God made me, and put me on a beach with a lot more like me, and he said, "There! Hold back the ocean!" And you know what? Together we do just that.

When it was time to leave Bonga, we were all looking forward to getting back to "civilization", but we were also sad to be leaving that place. I left most of my dresses for Rahab. Mom left whatever food we still had, and a lot of clothes and cooking things. Dad left his guitar with the boy who came to visit us so much, and Nathan left his most treasured possession: his basketball. In return, several of the boys gave Nathan a gift that he still treasures today: a set of throwing sticks, called "japante" in Uduk. One of the boys took Nathan aside and gave him some serious advice on their use. "Light weight ones.. for birds. Heavy ones.. for baboons. But remember, if you hunt baboons, you must always carry two japante. Baboons can count to two."

Since we live in Australia now, we compare those japante to Aboriginal boomerangs. But the only problem with a japante is, they don't come back like a boomerang. And just like a japante, I realized that we can probably never go back to Bonga. Politics and wars have made that part of the world a sad place to be. I often wonder where Rahab is, and if she's still alive. I hope she is, and I hope she's still singing "Jesus Loves Me".

Think about it:

The Uduk people should be an inspiration to all of us. They know what it's like to be killed for their faith, and to try and make a new home in a place that's not home. Even today, sourrounded by sickness, death, and hunger, they know how to laugh. And the reason is simple: they know Jesus. What more do you need to know?

This is the way; walk in it.   Isaiah 30:21

Chapter Seventeen

Moving on

*A*fter leaving Ethiopia, we visited family in America for a few weeks, and then made our way to the Missionary Learning Center in Richmond, Virginia (MLC). My parents were responsible for helping to orient new missionaries, so we got to live in an apartment on campus, and I started first grade again, this time as part of the missionary orientation program, run by the learning center.

We stayed at MLC for about four months. My best

friend there was a girl named Jasmine, who would be headed for Korea when her training was over. Korea's so close to Japan, she'd practically be my neighbor! My teacher was Miss Lisa, and we spent a lot of time making and eating all the American food we could get, with my parents grumbling about what they euphemistically referred to as 'Furlough Fat'. I was gaining weight as well, but that's to be expected for a healthy young girl.

Then we were off for another few months in Colorado where my dad did a pulpit exchange with a pastor who had gone to our church in Japan. You guessed it, I was sent to yet another first grade! I was beginning to be a pro at this first grade stuff.

When our stateside assignment was finished, we were off again, back to Japan, but first we were needed to stop in Australia for a month! Again, at the request of the mission board, we went to Sydney to 'check out' the Japanese work there.

An Australian congregation had approached the mission because they had a group of Japanese coming in the afternoons to worship and the Australians had no way of either communicating with them or knowing really who they were and what they were up to. Since we would be traveling 'that direction' towards Japan, it was decided that our family would stop and do this one last little job before returning home.

Again we were off to a new country. We were only to be there for a month, but I received a uniform and an invitation to join the first grade at the nearby primary school. This would be my fourth start , and I enjoyed it immensely, although my teacher was very frustrated that I couldn't read as well as the rest of the class.

I remember one day on the sidewalk in front of the school she was fussing at my Mom about this problem as my Mom shrugged her shoulders and said, "Well, she'll be back in Japanese school in a month, so English is not that important". The teacher stepped up closer and said right into her face, "Do you not wish her to be ELOQUENT?

I think my Mom was angry, but she just smiled and said, "Oh, I think I'd rather have her be BILINGUAL", and with that she took my hand and marched me home. I'm sure she was wondering why I couldn't be both bilingual AND eloquent in both languages.

Think about it:

Those words, "eloquent" and "bilingual" raise another question: what language does God speak? How do my stumbling attempts at prayer sound to His ears? Well, here's some good news, and it comes from Romans 8:26, "We don't know how to pray as we should, but the Spirit Himself intercedes for us with groanings too deep for words." Bottom line? It doesn't matter what language you speak, or how well you speak it. God's Holy Spirit, Who lives in the heart of every believer knows exactly what you want to say, and takes that prayer all the way to God's throne for you. So don't worry about it; just DO it!

I will never leave you nor forsake you   Joshua 1:5

Chapter Eighteen

Heading Home

*S*oon we were bound for Japan after a whole year of being away. We were arriving just in time for the new school year and I started... first grade again! It was a Japanese school, and I enjoyed it so much that I elected to stay in the first grade, even though I really should be in the second grade by now.

Let me explain. By the time we had been gone from Japan for a year, I had forgotten a lot of Japanese, so it was thought that if I started off in Japanese first grade

I could pick up my Japanese and then move into the second grade mid year.

We were now living in the little village of Nojiriko in the prefecture of Nagano, which was to be the site of the 1998 Winter Olympics. My parents were to be helping coordinate and organizing all the Christian volunteers who would be coming to work in the evangelical outreach, so that meant we needed to live there for at least a year before the Olympics began. So, first grade number five. As it turned out, this was my favorite one of them all.

The town where we lived in was about one hour from Nagano city and as it was a small farming community, the school was tiny. But as one of the only foreigners to ever go to that school, I was treated like a movie star! I especially loved my teacher, a man named Kobayashi Sensei.(teacher). God was going to use this man in an amazing way I'll tell you about in the next chapter. Suffice it to say here that I loved the man so much that I resolutely refused to move on to the second grade at mid year, preferring to stay behind if it meant staying with this awesome teacher. I had a great time and made lots of friends that year

What can I say? I guess doing the first grade five times wasn't too bad. After all, it was a real "well rounded" education: I got to learn to eat chicken feet and ride the Hong Kong ferries and subways, then I got to meet Rahab, learned how to grind corn and sing in ways most folks never do. I learned to sing "Jesus Loves Me" in three languages. But mostly, I learned that no matter where you go, God goes with you. He never forgets where you are, and always has just the right blessing at just the right time.

Think about it:

Moving from one place to another taught me that wherever I go and whatever I do, God will always be there. It doesn't matter where I am living, as long as I have Christ living in me. He doesn't let me fall. He never will. As long as I am in his hand I am safe. God's love for me will never change and it will never change for you either.

The earth is the Lord's, and everything in it, the world, and all who live in it...   Psalm 24:1

Chapter Nineteen

Surely Not Another Move!

$\mathcal{H}$ave you ever been faced with something really major that you didn't want to go through? Until I was eight years old, these kinds of things never really bothered me because, well, because I was little! Even the huge experience of leaving the orphanage was something I pretty much took in stride, just as any child would have. But as I grew older, I began to see the world around me, and I was loving it. Japan was turning out to be a great place, with lots of friends, great food and wonderful parents.

But then one day in 1998, I got the news that we were going to be moving to Australia just as soon as the school year and the winter Olympics were over. I had absolutely no idea why this sudden decision had been made, but I found out later that my parents had been praying about the move ever since our visit to Australia a year ago. They were to tell me later that this was perhaps the hardest decision they had ever made, because it first felt like they might be abandoning Japan. However, as they prayed about it, they realized that their work in Australia would perhaps make even a greater impact on Japan eventually.

Japanese in Australia are really more open to the Gospel and have fewer resources to help them, so my folks wanted to move there and be missionaries. I'll have to say, I was getting old enough to have an opinion and this time I didn't like the idea.

This was my first experience at what missionary kids all over the world were going through. There are heaps of papers and books written about what is called "Third Culture Kids or TCKs, meaning that you're a child who had no culture that is entirely yours, except for that 'third culture' that says you don't really fit anywhere. It's not a bad thing, but just a thing that
114

I was becoming. As "missionaries" my mom and dad were expected to move a lot, always going where God sent them, which could be anywhere, from Africa to Asia to …. Australia. Altogether by now, our family has moved five or six times, not counting at least that many extended trips to America for what's known as "deputation". Old missionaries used to say "furlough" but that means a rest, and it's anything but that. Now, in fact, the younger missionaries call it "stateside assignment" which is probably a more correct term.

For a lot of missionaries, deputation means going from church to church and enlisting support for the work they do. My parents are Southern Baptist missionaries, which means they're supported by a cooperative program and don't raise individual support, but they do need to visit as many churches as they can, thanking them for being a part of the system that enables them to do what they do, and helping them to see what God's doing all over the world.

Anyway, you might think I was used to moving around, but leaving Japan was a tough experience, taking over three months from the time we started packing until we had finally moved into a new home "Down Under". It was a time in my life where God tested my faith, for

115

real.

First, we had to pack up, and that meant major cleaning. Our family had only been in the house they were leaving for five years, but it was the only real home I had ever known. Digging through drawers, closets and boxes, we discovered things we didn't even know we had. And besides our house in Taitomi, we had a little cabin up in the mountains where we went every year for vacation, and it was a mess! Then there was another mission house over in the city of Nagano where we had set up temporary quarters so my Dad could direct the volunteers during the 1998 Winter Olympics. It was full of stuff, too, like lots of bedding, furniture, left over Olympic stuff, and heaps of winter clothes that we'd never need again.

It took a long, long time, but finally everything was stuffed into a crate to be sent to Australia. Well, almost everything. The crate was so full that when we got to the last pair of skis, there was no place for them to go, so we gave them to the neighbors. Seeing the truck drive away with everything that I had called home was pretty hard on me. My parents kept telling me that we'd see those things again, but I still cried.

Then there was our dog, a little Sheltie collie whose name was Girl. When I first saw her, I was so scared. I don't think I'd ever seen one at the orphanage, except in pictures. It took awhile, but she finally won me over. We have videos of me playing with her as a three-year-old. I almost feel sorry for her, to see how I treated her like a rag doll. But she was patient with me, and we soon became great friends. At first, my parents thought we couldn't take her to Australia, but my brother and I both were so upset, they finally agreed to see what they could do. For weeks ahead of time, we had to take her to the vet for shots and so he could insert a tiny computer chip under her skin (required by Australian law). Then, we took her to the airport, checked her in and left her sitting in a little cage, looking confused and forlorn. That was so hard on all of us! Even after she got to Australia, she had to be quarantined for a month, and we weren't even allowed to visit her. I couldn't help feeling that maybe she must have felt a lot like I did.

Think about it:

I think what surprised Mom and Dad the most about this latest move was the fact that, for the first time, I had an opinion about it. When you're younger, you just sort of "go with the flow", even if it flows halfway around the world. With the years, though, comes an increasing recognition of the world you live in, and some definite ideas about where you call home. Maybe that's why Heaven is such a great place ... in theory. I mean, I do want to go there, but as I look around at the place I call home today, the idea of leaving it just doesn't carry the thrill it used to. And as I think about it, maybe that's partly why Jesus said we need to "become like children" to see the Kingdom of Heaven (Matthew 18:3). Okay Lord, as much as I love growing up, help me hold onto the childlike things that keep me longing to be with You.

He put a new song in my mouth, a hymn of praise
to our God   Psalm 40:3

Chapter Twenty

Sydney, Australia

*M*oving to Australia meant not only leaving Japan, but also leaving behind lifelong friends (at least as lifelong as an eight-year-old can have) and saying goodbye to all the "Japanese" things I had learned to love. Like going into a restaurant and hearing "irrrashimase!" (Welcome!) from all the employees. We used to make it a game, to try and leave the store without everyone noticing us and shouting out "arigatou gozaimasu!!" (thank you for coming!). Things like taking our shoes off whenever we go inside anywhere, even at church. and always remembering to bow to everyone. All of these customs and memories would now be left behind.

Looking back, those things now seem kind of strange, but back then, it was the world I had learned to love, and I hated to leave it behind. Could my life get any worse? I wondered. First I had to leave the orphanage, and now I had to leave here. What would I have to do next? Why had God done this to us? Maybe He wasn't the wonderful God I had come to think of whenever I thought of Him.

From my earliest memories there in Japan, I had heard people saying, "You know, Nicki is always going to people who are crying." This had a big effect on me, and even now, I think that helping others is a part of the call that God is giving me. As we packed up to leave the house for the last time though, I wiped a few tears from my eyes and thought, "Okay God; now it's my turn."

Arriving in Sydney, we got our first taste of missionary life in a country where there is no Baptist mission family. A couple of Aussie pastors met us at the airport, but instead of a big welcome, they knew we'd be tired so they just gave us the keys to a rental car and showed us on the map where we were supposed to go, which was a caravan park across town.

I think in a way my parents were real glad not to have to go straight to a big party, because we'd been working so hard and then had been on the plane all night, so they just wanted to go to bed. But still, it was sort of lonely, especially after I was getting used to being the center of attention in Japan.

We moved into a caravan, or a house trailer, as they say in America, and it was small! We had to look for our own house to rent, and the mission had strict guide-lines, so it would be three months in this trailer before our crates came and we could move into a real house. In a way, it was a good experience, because our family got to know each other real well!

But I was still upset with God. Was He putting me through some kind of test and if I passed it, then could I go back to Japan? Why was all this happening, any-way? At the age of eight, I just couldn't appreciate that we were here because God was sending us to Japanese living in Australia.

In a way, they were the crying people that I was looking for. They were away from home, too, and a lot of them didn't speak English, and a lot of them (especially the kids) didn't want to be there either. The only difference was, most of them didn't know God, and so had nowhere to turn. I didn't know it yet, but this was going to be one of my biggest challenges: to reach out to other kids like myself, and help them find a home away from home.

My mom and dad found my brother a school to go to close to where we lived. He had finished the tenth grade and now was having to jump back into the middle of the tenth grade again since the school year starts in February in Australia. I was also having to start in the middle of the second grade, even though I had only just begun, in April, the second grade in Japan. In other words, he was starting sort of behind where he'd finished and I was jumping ahead. It took him awhile to get settled in, and whereas I was pretty excited about my new uniform, he hated his. He was also surprised to find a difference in attitude towards students from the American based education he'd had in Japan to British based education. It was certainly a shock, but fortunately, he was old enough to get his learner's permit and start driving, so that cheered him up and eventually he began to relax. Within a few months he was able to find some great friends that he still keeps up with today.

Think about it:

The move to Sydney was a major step for me to take. It was a step I didn't really have a say in but it was step that God took with me. Traveling around is always a big step but actually moving to a foreign country is always different. There's so many more things you have to do than just traveling. God always helps me get over my culture shock and He never forgets to help me to settle into a new home. People ask me where is my home and most of the time my answer is America, but I've never actually really lived there. When I am in America I always say Australia is home but I lived in Japan the longest. So where is home exactly? Well for now and always it's with God.

Apply your heart to instruction and your ears to words of knowledge   Proverbs 23:12

Chapter Twenty One

Mr Kobayashi Goes to a New School

$\mathcal{B}$ut what about me? So far, I had only been to one kind of school in my life: Japanese school (except for the short times at all those other first grades). Everything else had all been in Japanese, taught by Japanese. Coming to Australia, my parents knew that I would have to get into the Australian system soon, but in order to help with the transition; they first enrolled me in the Sydney Japanese School.

It was an official branch school run by the government of Japan for those who needed to continue in an accredited Japanese school system. This meant that it had the same textbooks and curriculum that kids back in Japan study. They even use Japanese teachers, transferring them to their schools all over the world for two years at a time, again so that the children who attend these schools will face as little transition issues as possible.

Now I want to share with you something just amazing.

Do you remember me talking about my last school I went to in Japan, where I refused to leave the first grade because I loved the teacher so much? It was in a small town near Nagano city, but up in the mountains at a place called Nojiri. The town was a small country village, and the little school was perfect for a girl like me: big enough to have all the friends I could handle, and small enough so that everyone knew everyone else.

But my favorite thing of all was my first grade teacher, Mr. Kobayashi. He was the first man teacher I had known, unless you consider the Russian doctor, Dr. Vegislav back at the orphanage, and maybe that was why I liked him so much. He was full of enthusiasm for his class, and whether he was teaching us how to do math or how to cross country ski out in the play ground, he always managed to get us excited about it. I loved him.

It was near the end of the school year, and I knew that we would be leaving for Australia soon. My mom and I had gone to school one day before class started because we needed to do whatever it is people do just before leaving for good. As we walked up to the school, though, I saw a lot of my classmates coming out onto the playground, and they were all crying! "Doshita no?" (What's wrong?,) I asked.

"Mr. Kobayashi is leaving!" they cried.

"Leaving?" I exclaimed. "Why? What happened? Where is he going?"

"He's been transferred to Sydney, Australia!"

It was hard for me to cry that day with the rest of my friends (although I did try to look suitably sad for everyone!). All I could think was, Mr. Kobayashi is going to be a teacher at the same school I'll be going to in Australia! My parents were shocked as well, and my dad even went to see the principal of the school. "How did Mr. Kobayashi arrange this?" he asked the principal. "We haven't told anyone before today we're going to Australia. Did Mr. Kobayashi know we were moving to Sydney?"

"No," said the principal. "He had no choice in the matter. He was simply transferred. If he's going to the same place you are, then it was just a coincidence." Some coincidence.

When we got to Sydney, my parents enrolled me at the Sydney Japanese School. Soon after we met Mr. Kobayashi and his family, who had just moved down to Australia a month earlier to begin the new school year. He was assigned to teach the fifth grade, while I would be placed in the second grade. I was disappointed at that, but his classroom was right across the hall from me, so every time the bell would ring ending the class, I would rush to the door and call out, "Kobayashi Sensei? Imasu ka?" "Mr. Kobayashi! Are you there?" He would come out smiling and I would give him a deep bow and we would talk, laugh, and share stories about the new experience we were both having. That year went a whole lot better because he was there.

Think about it:

Mr. Kobayashi was a great teacher. He inspired his students to enjoy their time at school. His move to Australia to work at the same Japanese school I attended was nothing less than God seeing to it that I made the transition to Australia with a minimum of difficulty. I think too that God had His hand on Mr. Kobayashi, helping him to experience first hand God's work in his own life. By the time he and his family returned to Japan, they still hadn't made a commitment to Christ, but I believe they will. And I still pray for him. I pray that the talent God has given him for teaching and influencing young children like me will be put to use for God's Kingdom. Remember to pray for your teachers today. Thank God for the ones who teach because of their love for God and His call to them. And pray for those who haven't heard that call yet.

Do not forsake wisdom, and she will protect you; love her, and she will watch over you   Proverbs 4:6

Chapter Twenty Two

Getting My Education Going

J finished out the second grade at Sydney Japanese School, then went into the third grade. It was the perfect transition for me, coming into a whole new culture and home in Australia, but having familiar friends and studies and even my favorite teacher close by.

By the third grade, I was feeling more at home in Australia, and was beginning to make lots of Aussie friends. My parents decided it was time to take another step of transition, and so for the third grade, they moved me from the purely Japanese system to the international system that was within the Japanese school. It met at the same place, but the classes were made up of kids from lots of different countries. Some of them had one Japanese parent and one parent from another country. Some were Japanese who had lived out of Japan so long they were more comfortable in an international environment. We still spoke Japanese a lot in class, but also a lot of English, and the curriculum was a little more English-based.

This was good for me, because by now I was starting to have trouble keeping up with the Japanese reading and writing. The Japanese language has three alphabets: a phonetic one for Japanese words, and another different but still phonetic one for all the foreign words that have been added into the Japanese vocabulary like "tabulu" (table) and "Ma-ko-donalu-doz" (MacDonalds). Of course the real BIG alphabet isn't an alphabet at all but Chinese characters or pictographs called "Kanji". There are about 40,000 possible words made up of these kanji. These kanji are not phonetic and must be just memorized, because they all have several completely different pronounciations depending on how they are used in the word. Obviously if you don't

130

study and use them every day, you start falling behind in reading. That's exactly what was happening with me.

Now, switching from Japanese schooling to English schooling is not easy, especially because my reading and writing of the English language was just horrible as well. Someone has said that the first three years of education are the hardest in regards to learning English, because it is a language of exceptions, which must also be memorized in order to read well. I did manage it, though, and was able to get through my studies with some effort.

Now in addition I began to have other challenges; it was like God was saying, "Okay Nicki, it's time to go to work."

Think about it:

"Change" is a word that describes my life. I've gone through so many different things. I guess the reason my life is so different is because of the change in my life. This is one major thing I thank God for. Think about it. If you always did the same thing throughout your whole life would you really enjoy it? I guess God made different plans for people so it would be fun and enjoyable. For me I move a lot. I've always moved and I guess I kind of enjoy that but the one thing that was really hard was changing school systems all the time. It wasn't easy going from Japan, to America, back to Japan then to Australia. The schooling systems are way different. I started the first grade so many times I was a pro and now I realized that God gave me that experience firstly so that one I would be so familiar with the first grade that I could probably do it again now and secondly so I that I could have the experience of the first grade in so any different places. I thank God for that every day. Start enjoying the changes in your life even if they are hard. They're put there just for you.

...be as shrewd as snakes and as innocent as doves

Matthew 10:16

Chapter Twenty Three

Using My Head

a girl at my school used to always steal my lunch, and I hated it. Yet I still liked her and wanted to be friends. I guess you might wonder how this could happen day after day, but there is a custom in most Japanese schools that when the lunch bell rings, the teacher leaves the classroom for the lunch hour and the kids remain to fend for themselves. I guess they figure the teacher needs a break, but sometimes it's hard on particular kids if there's bullying going on. Anyway, even though my parents complained, nothing was done.

One day I decided that I would be a very smart child and stop being a victim and just change my circumstances. Every day I made a sandwich from Nutella (a chocolate paste, much like peanut butter) and I suddenly realized that this might be why she was stealing it so consistently, so I hatched a devious plan. I switched my sandwich from Nutella to Vegemite (an Australian delicacy that must be experienced because it just can't be described!). It looks just like chocolate spread on the sandwich, but the taste sure isn't chocolate, but more like very salty yeast, and I have to say I still hadn't completely acquired a taste for it. Well, the first day after she stole that vegemite sandwich, she never bothered my lunches again!

But she was still a troubled girl, and seemed to go out of her way to pick on me and others. It was amazing to see the things she would come up with to hurt people. She didn't really like me but I never let that get in the way of how I treated her. Whenever she told me that she hated me because I spoke Japaneses better than she did, I would remind her that I'd spent most of my life in Japan so in a way it couldn't be helped. I would always tell her that I was willing to study with her and help her get better, but she would just walk away.

By the next year, as I was falling more and more behind in my English acquisition, my parents decided that it might be that I was ready to go into an Australian school, and so I was moved once more across town to a real nice Christian school closer to home. And guess what? That girl was moved to the same school!

God had something in mind for me to do with her; I was sure of it; I just didn't know what it was yet. In fact, I still don't know. At first I was pretty distraught, but when she moved into the new school, she seemed to settle right in and leave me alone. Who knows why I had to endure this time with her. In fact, she left that school after only six months and I lost track of her, but I think of her from time to time and hope she found God somewhere in all her unhappiness. Maybe some things I said will come back to her one day, and she'll change from a troubled, mean girl to a sweet child of God. Will I ever know if she does? I hope so.

Think about it:

Right on the heels of Mr. Kobayashi being transferred to the same school I was moving to, I then was given the experience of having my own personal bully transferred to another school at the same time I was moving there. Looking back, I can't help but believe that God had a part in both moves, but so far, I can't see what the outcome was, or I should say, what it will be. Mr. Kobayashi didn't become a Christian, and the bully remained a bully. But you see, that's part of how God works in our lives, isn't it? We catch glimpses of some amazing stuff going on, then we lose sight of it before everything is worked out. Life is not a television sitcom, where all issues are settled in 30 minutes or less. Life is what God has set us into, and while we know that things will all work together for good eventually, we're not always allowed to see that good. That calls for faith, and sometimes, a lot of it.

Dear friends, let us love one another, for love comes from God   1 John 4:7

Chapter Twenty Four

A New School

J have always told myself that any new experience should be a great experience, if for no other reason than the fact that it's new. With that philosophy in place, the New Year which brings in a New Millennium should, by definition, be fantastic! As it turned out, so many things happened with the opening of the year 2000, that I believe I became more of what I am now during that time than at any other time before or since.

Now as I look back, one thing is quite clear: God laid all these new things before me, and led me through them for His purposes. Experiencing them introduced me to a whole range of emotions, from anger to fear to absolute joy. And in every one of them, God's faithful Presence was the one thing I knew I could always count on.

The new year's journey with God began during the school summer holidays in 1999. As I mentioned before, my parents and I made the decision that I should move from the Japanese school to a full time Australian English speaking school. To be honest, I don't know exactly how I felt about it all. I mean, on the one hand, I was happy about the idea of going to a new place, and I was game to give it a try, but still, it would be a big change from what I knew and understood. However, as much as I enjoyed the Japanese school and all the reminders of what I was still missing back "home" in Japan, I think I was ready to move on to a world where I knew I could finally belong.

Even at that age, it was becoming more and more clear that I would always be a "gaijin" (foreigner) among these teachers and friends whom I loved so much. Japanese are among the kindest, most generous people on earth, but they also have a very strict sense of "us" and "them". To my Japanese friends, I would always be "them", and a part of me hurt to understand that fact. But as excited as I was about the new opportunities that lay ahead, I knew in my heart that this was going to be a major step away from the Japanese culture I had grown up in and had learned to love so dearly. I felt that if I left this school, I would be leaving a part of my life: a part that I wasn't sure I could ever go back to.

For many of my friends, this would be the watershed moment, when all their secret doubts about me were finally confirmed. They would know, once and for all, that I really was a 'gaijin', and had no future in their world.

Fortunately for me, I didn't have to think about it too much, since the final decision was, after all, in the hands of my parents. They thought about it, prayed about it, and finally decided that it would be best for me to go into the Australian school. I probably complained a little on the outside, but deep inside I was happy.

I didn't know exactly what to expect at the new school, but I had visions of lots of kids who looked just like me, and days filled with just doing what everyone else was doing, without the constant fear of being different. So, as the year 2000 began and I walked into my new school, I was filled with excitement and anticipation.

I was starting fourth grade at Beachview Grammar School in Sydney. It was a beautiful school, and I fell in love with it right away. My new teacher's name was Mr. Love, so I figured with a name like that, he had to be great! And he was. He took a special interest in me right away, helping me fit into a new situation with as little drama as possible. Mr. Love taught me a lot of new skills that year, both in my studies and in sports that I had never had a chance to learn before. I soon discovered that I could run fairly well, and since Mr. Love was also the track coach, he spent a lot of time showing me the fundamentals and helping me fit into a whole new group of girls: the athletes. And with this new-found popularity, I discovered that my expectations of finding new friends was going to be everything I dreamed it would be.

After two months in Beachview Grammar school, it seemed like I had made friends with just about everyone in the school. Being more or less "normal", at least on the outside, no one had any issues with me, and seemed to welcome me right into their circles of friends. Before long, though, I started to discover that there was another level of friendship which I had never known. Opening that door proved to be a painful experience.

Back in Japan, I had gotten used to being "different", and as such never quite finding total acceptance with other girls. At Beachview Grammar, I learned that being a foreigner is not the only reason some people are left on the outside.

Think about it:

If you have ever been in a situation where you are judged for the way you are or the way you act. I know how you feel. Fitting into a new school hasn't always been easy for me but with God's help and encouraging parents I've somehow been able to fit in. A girl in my grade didn't exactly think that I was a nice person at all. I don't know why. When she confronted me about who I hang out with I was hurt. I wasn't happy about the whole situation, but I did get through that year. I was just myself. Without God, it would have been a lot harder than it was. It's during your hard times that he carries you.

141

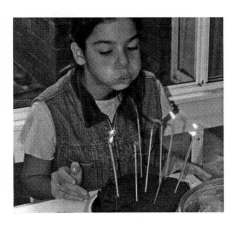

Man looks at the outward appearance, but God looks at the heart   1 Samuel 16:7

Chapter Twenty Five

Finding Friends

*W*ithin the first week of school, before I'd made any real friends, I met a girl in my class, and I got to know her better when we were paired up to do an assignment together. She was a really nice girl, but she suffered from a slight physical disability in one arm. Unfortunately, this was the first thing that most people noticed about her, and in some cases, the only thing. She was often the victim of cruel teasing, or

142

even worse, was totally ignored. My heart went out to her, because I saw so much of myself in her. I didn't have a physical disability that you could see, but everybody has something they can't do and as I began watching her try so hard to be a part of things, only to be shunned or laughed at, I really felt her pain.

But it wasn't just pity that made me want to be her friend. She really was a sweet girl, with a lot to offer to anyone who would listen. I found myself spending more and more time with her, both at school and at each other's homes. We must have seen that special bond right away, and enjoyed our time together.

Eventually, one of my other new friends came to me during lunch time. "Nicki," she said, "I'm telling you this as a friend. We all like you and want you to be a part of our group. But we all know that that girl is embarrassing to be around. You need to understand that if you keep hanging out with her, you won't have any friends here at Beachview Grammar." I was speechless, so she went on. "It's nothing personal, Nicki. I'm just telling you the facts. You're going to have to choose: either give her up, or give up the rest of us."

As my supposed "friend" sauntered off away to join

the other "in crowd" of girls, I thought, "What am I supposed to do?" Go and tell my first new friend, one that except for an unusable arm is as fine a girl as you'd want to meet, "Sorry, but I have to ignore you now. It's nothing personal."

I'd been taught in Sunday school to be kind and generous to everyone, especially the "poor in spirit." Who was the real poor in spirit here: this girl or those "friends" who were being so cruel? I know it sounds silly, looking back on the situation now, but it wasn't an easy decision to make. I loved having my new cool crowd, and dreaded the thought of going back to the way it was before I'd come to this school, with me not fitting in, being on the outside again. At the time, I really didn't know what to do.

I thought about it all weekend, and by the time Monday morning came around, I had decided that I would be strong and do the right thing. Deciding was the easy part; following through on my decision was one of the toughest things I ever had to do. I felt like I just didn't have the strength to say what needed to be said. The temptation was so strong to go over to the handicapped girl instead and tell her that we just couldn't be friends anymore. She would be disappointed, but she'd get over it. After all, I was sure that she'd been through this kind of thing before. She would go on with her life, I'd still have my other friends, and things would be fine. "God, give me strength," I prayed.

Lunch time came, and I was still debating about what to do when the girl who had talked to me on Friday came up.

"So what have you decided to do?" she asked.

"God loves everyone," I said. "Even you. This girl can't help the way she is, and when I think about it, you can't help the way you are, either. I'm not going to stop hanging out with her just because you and the girls say I should. If you can't deal with that, then I guess we can't be friends."

It was a hard choice to make, I admit it. And I'd like to say that everyone saw it my way and we all lived happily ever after, but that's not the case. I did lose a lot of potential friends with that decision, although I have to say that I picked up a few new ones, and better ones at that. I can only hope that some day those other girls will begin to understand what they did, and maybe feel sorry and maybe even become better friends to someone else some day.

I think I came away knowing one thing: if I had listened to them and done what they were demanding of me, I wouldn't have been a very good friend to myself, nor to Jesus. The scary thing is that I really had to think about that decision for a long time.

I really don't know what came over me that day. Sitting there listening to this girl telling me to trash a friendship for the sake of other friends, something inside me really wanted to do what they said. At the same time, God kept telling me what I knew all along was the right thing to do, and finally I paid attention and saw that He was right. But it didn't come easy.

Perhaps, as I mentioned earlier, "change" is a word that describes my life. I've gone through so many changes, and I believe that my life is different because of them. The move to Australia was one of the biggest changes of all, and I think my trust in God helped me get through the experience. I mentioned that a lot of people helped me throughout my life, teaching me how to live and love life. I now know that at this point in my life when I go through hard times just to rely on God and He will create an easier or more meaningful path for me to walk on. I know that at the low points of your life you feel as though God isn't with you. You feel alone and rejected. I felt the same way. I just want to share this with you: it's the hard times in life that bring you to hard choices. And the hard choices lead you into whole new places where God wants to take you. When I had my first birthday in Australia, I was surprised to even have friends there. I mean, just to have people show up was amazing. I thought I was all alone. But I wasn't alone then, and I'm not now. You just have to rely on God, and He'll show you things you never expected, especially during times of change.

Think about it:

Finding friends has not always been easy. During the year God showed me a verse that I have loved and treasured forever and this is what it says: Proverbs 17:17, A friend loves at all times and a brother is born for a difficult time. This verse spoke to me as I have a best friend and a brother. I love them both at all times. It's an encouraging verse that helps me get through hard times when I just don't feel loved. It expresses that we are loved, at all times.

Commit to the Lord whatever you do, and your plans will succeed   Proverbs 16:3

Chapter Twenty Six

Knowing How it Feels to Work Hard

𝒯he year 2000 was marked by the summer Olympic Games, held in Sydney, Australia. But for me, the new year brought with it so much more in the way of new experiences as I have mentioned in the last chapter, some enjoyable, some definitely more challenging. For one thing, my school work was getting more difficult, to the point that my parents thought they should have me tested for learning disabilities.

What we discovered was a shock, but looking back, I don't suppose that it was much of a surprise. The diagnosis was "classic" ADHD, or "Attention Deficit Hyperactivity Disorder". I say it wasn't particularly surprising, because by the time I was well into second grade, words like "live wire", "fidget" and "sugar high" were used to describe me. The doctors were quick to point out, though, that ADHD is not a disease, but simply a condition, shared by such highly successful notables as Winston Churchill. It was even said that people with ADHD make the best airplane pilots, since they can watch the whole instrument panel simultaneously, while carrying on a conversation and looking out the window, instead of focusing on just one thing at a time.

I'm pretty sure that my "condition" did challenge my school mates, though, since I tended to be pretty "up close and in your face" all day long. When it came to studies, I was impossible. I mean, who can sit still and read a book when there are so many other things demanding your attention? My parents looked into several treatments, but nothing seemed right for me. They even considered Ritalin, the drug of choice for many kids with ADHD, and tried it for awhile as a "blind study", giving it to me in the morning along with my vitamins.

After a couple of months, they met with my teachers and were amused to find that all the ones who had me in their morning classes said that I was a perfect angel, while the afternoon class teachers had a quite different description! Ritalin might be the answer for some kids, they concluded, but decided to seek other options for me. What they found was a relatively new approach at that time, called "Neurometric Feedback".

It was interesting, to say the least, and involved using a computer with sensors attached to my head and then tied into a computer. By concentrating really hard, I could actually make things happen on the computer screen, just using my 'brain power'. For example a face would start smiling or a bird would start singing when I thought intently about the task. When my mind began to drift, things would stop, and I would know that I needed to get back with the program.

It took several months of practice, but eventually I was able to read a book sitting in front of the computer while cartoon characters ran across the monitor, singing and dancing and assuring me that I was "in the groove". Eventually, my school work began to improve
150

as my reading got better, and that helped in a whole lot of ways. I think I'm still a little ADHD today, but with the proper controls, it's actually a good thing, letting me "multitask" on several projects at once.

What was I talking about? Oh yes, the Sydney Olympics. Here was a unique opportunity to occupy my active mind. At the Nagano Winter Olympics, I had been able to get involved a little with my parents as they coordinated the volunteer workers coming to both the Olympics and Paralympics, but I had only been eight at the time. Now, in the year 2000, I was ready and willing to get involved in the volunteer program in Sydney. Once again, my folks were working with the volunteers, so I had plenty of opportunity to take part. I helped pass out programs, guided people through the city's attractions, traded Olympic pins and even translated for some of the Japanese visitors.

It was special, to say the least, but I have to say, I enjoyed working with the Paralympic athletes most of all. For them, "personal best" takes on a whole new meaning. I mean, it's one thing to run a hundred yard dash, but how would you like to do it with only one leg? Rugby is a vicious sport, but try playing it while sitting in a wheelchair! I grew to really admire and respect those men and women who could overcome their disabilities and accomplish so much. I don't know, maybe that experience helped prepare me for my first real friend (whom I talked about in the last chapter).

But clearly the best thing about the year 2000 was overcoming my own "attention deficit" challenge and finishing fourth grade with flying colors. My first day in the fifth grade felt as if my faith was running low. My English was still a little rusty, and the studies were definitely getting more difficult. I think this was the year I discovered books, though, and that contributed more to my progress than anything else. Short stories, long stories, fiction, non-fiction, picture books and even science and math books: it was like a whole new world had been opened to me, a world which had always been there but because of the combination of poor English and ADHD, it was a world I had never really stepped into until now.

Think about it:

I guess to some people if I told them that I had ADHD they wouldn't believe me. But it's true. God gave this to me and as a little kid I use to drive my parents crazy. I guess that's why they love me so much. Overcoming it was my main goal and I did. Eventually I finally started to concentrate in class, listen to my friend's speak and not just zone out when watching a movie. I was really upset that I had it as a little girl and I don't think my parents were that happy either but God did bring me some thing good out of it. It meant that I could do like three things at once. And for that I was grateful.

*You broaden the path beneath me, so that my ankles do
not turn*   Psalm 18: 36

Chapter Twenty Seven

Stepping Out

𝒯hen one day I stepped a little too far – over a boy's
outstretched foot actually – and crashed to the ground,
breaking my ankle. He insists that he didn't trip me
on purpose, and I'll choose to believe that, but you all
know how grade five boys can be. As it turned out,
it was more than a simple break, and actually a case
of bad timing, in that the bone snapped just before it
had stopped growing and calcified. The doctor told us
154

that if it had been three months later, the bone could have taken it, and I would have just had a bad sprain but instead I spent several hours in surgery and had to get a couple of screws to fix it back in place. It was quite funny, because when my Mom was called to the nurse's desk, she asked if she thought it was broken, "Oh certainly not," said the nurse. "If it was broken, she'd be screaming!". Guess that shows you what a tough little cookie I am!

To make matters worse, our family was two weeks away from a trip back to the States for deputation, with stops to visit some Japanese ministries in South America as well. I was on crutches the whole time, which in some ways was good, since people occasionally took pity on me, like at the airports, etc, but generally it was a literal pain. I did get to climb up to Macchu Pichu, but it took a while on crutches!

One thing the experience accomplished for me, though, was to give me a lasting respect for those Paralympic athletes I had just been spending time with. "So this is what it means to be unable to do the things I really, really wanted to do", I thought to myself. It was a big temptation to drop down into a "pity party" and bask in everyone's sympathy, but whenever I felt myself going there, I'd have to stop and say, "Wait a minute! You're not so bad off, you know. In six weeks, you'll be off these crutches, and as good as new.

Some of those men and women whom you now call friends will NEVER get any better than they are right now. And how do they deal with it? They go to the Olympics!" I decided then and there that I would use this time of "disability" to try and see the world through their eyes. What I discovered were some things that I didn't expect to find. Like the fact that a person's physical disability is not the only part of his or her life. I mean, when you see a disabled person on the street, that may be the first thing that comes to your mind, but what do you suppose that person is thinking about? Certainly not the disability, not 24/7. All of God's creation have been blessed with all kinds of gifts, and if we miss seeing those because we can't see past some physical handicap, then who's the blind one?

Coming back home to Australia and losing my crutches, I felt like I was ready to start being "normal". Problem was, I wasn't sure what "normal" was supposed to be. It was certainly never a word used to describe me! Year six was beginning, and I soon found that my studies were becoming easier, probably because the
156

ADHD thing was under control. My friendship with the disabled girl was more relaxed and enjoyable too, and we both discovered that our classmates were becoming more mature in their attitudes as well. Kids who used to tease me for being friends with her, now struck up conversations with us and acted as if they really wanted to know us both. By now, I had pretty much determined that I wanted to do the right thing more than I wanted to be accepted by everyone; and in the process I found that by doing the right thing consistently brought more acceptance than ever before.

I guess you could say that this year was a major year emotionally for me. I finally got to experience some true happiness. I started to actually enjoy my studies and becoming an 'A' student was now my new goal. I knew that this goal wouldn't just come to me overnight but as I prayed, put a smile on my face and looked at life differently I started to have dreams of what I actually wanted to do in life. Grade six was going to be the year for real friends, real achievements and real growth. I was excited and ready to roll.

Extracurricular activities caught my eye that year, and I decided to find something I could be good at. In America, I had watched boys playing basketball with my brother, but for some reason it never occurred to me that girls could play too. Then one day at school, I noticed a group of high school girls playing basketball. It was then and there that I said to myself "I have another dream, basketball. I want to play basketball!" I asked around and found that there was an after school girls' basketball club. I checked it out, joined up, and soon was playing my heart out every week. I won't say I was especially good at it. In fact, I'm not sure if we ever won a game, but it was a real highlight of the week. Getting to know the girls on the team was a real plus, and when we shared a happy moment or a disappointment, it just drew us closer together.

Think about it:

It's not just during the hard times that I rely on God but it's also the times I'm in pain. I broke my ankle during the fifth grade and I have to say that God helped me through every medical process. He was with me when I was getting the screw put into my ankle and when I was getting them taken out as well. I knew then that God did truly love me. Trusting him hasn't always been easy and I've come to realize that it's when we need him most that we fully rely on him. We need to rely on him even when we don't need him. Thank Him for the good things in life and always look to him for everything.

When I was a child, I talked like a child, I thought like a child, I reasoned like a child   1 Corinthians 13: 12

Chapter Twenty Eight

Growing Up

*A*nother great part of grade six was becoming a teenager. For my 13th birthday, my parents gave me a "Purity" ring and I loved it. It represents a vow that I've made that until the day I get married I will be pure. Engraved on the outside are the words, "True Love Waits". The famous American singer, who is actually a transplanted Australian, Rebecca St. James, had begun to support the "True Love Waits" campaign at her Australian concerts, so I was immediately quite 'cool' to have my own ring and pledge. Now, looking at it, I'm reminded that a lot of life is all about waiting, even when we're not aware of it. Until the age of three, I was waiting for my family to come to Russia and get me. We waited and waited for passports, visas, citizenship and all kinds of other things. Some of the waiting was easy, while some was a real "patience tester". But one thing I'm beginning to see is this: all waiting does eventually come to an end. My family did come; my papers did arrive; and in God's time, my true love will find me. My grandmother used to say one of the greatest promises in the Bible was the little phrase, "And it came to pass". I guess while I wait for all these things to happen in my life, I might as well enjoy what I have and make the most of it.

You could say that it was just luck to have a good year but I don't think it was luck. I think it was God. He seemed to have his hand over me the whole year. Even during the rough times that I thought God wasn't there. It was then that he was carrying me. During the sixth grade I felt more and more that He was right there by my side every day..

After the school holidays I started high school at the same school. My disabled friend had moved on to another school and I wished her well. Wherever she is now I hope that God has his hand on her. I always had fun having her as a friend and I thank her for being such a good friend to me.

My first day of high school was a little nerve racking. What first day of school isn't? I've had so many first days of school, so why was I so nervous about this one? Maybe it was the new uniform, complete with a high school blazer and tie, or maybe it was just knowing that High School would carry so much more responsibility. Anyway, as I was standing near the secondary office of the high school area I saw some of the new girls that I had met at the orientation morning breakfast for all the seventh graders. I spotted two girls that I remembered from that breakfast and went over to them. I introduced myself and from then on we became close friends. I had a good feeling about these two and I had fun hanging out with them at school.

One of them, Blythe, started out a little shy. Me being so out going and wanting to have friends, I think at first she kind of thought that I was a little weird, but as the year went on I think she came to realize that I wasn't too bad to be around. She even started to come out of her shell and being a bit silly herself some times, having crazy and fun moments with me. I guess I have that impact on people.

Another girl new to the school was a girl named Rebecca, and we soon all started calling her Bec. Well, I guess you could say that she knew from the beginning that I was really weird and out there. So I think we hit it off like that and have been good friends ever since.

Grade seven was so much fun. I thought that it was interesting that some of the girls who didn't exactly favor me in primary school started to come around a little bit. Remember I said that I thought they might grow up a bit, and I guess they did. One of them in particular I still had some convincing to do but bit by bit I was getting there. As God was showing me new things this year and bringing special people into my life to help me through the first year of my high school life I was happy that I was doing pretty well.

Throughout grade seven and eight I was pretty "normal". Nothing major bad happened, no broken bones, no broken hearts, no nothing. During these years I became very close to an old friend. Her name is Charity Emi Gierhart and she's always been a girl of faith and cheerfulness and has helped me through my good times and my bad times. Remember how I stayed with the family in Hawaii when I was three and waiting for my citizenship? Well, Charity is the sister in that family, and through an interesting set of circumstances, their family also made their way from Japan to work with Japanese in Australia, so in a way, the Gierharts are our only 'Family' in Australia. I guess I can say that she's the sister I never actually had.

I grew up not living anywhere close to her in Japan but when we moved to Australia she became a friend who was there for me, even when I felt like the world around me was just crumbling down. Now she lived only five minutes away by car, and as our families were together a lot. We became close friends. She always comforted me with kind words and always knew how to make a bad situation into a good positive one. She even knew how to make me smile and to this day all I can say to her is "I love you".

Think about it:

Do you think there will be babies in Heaven? I don't think so, and that's because God wants us to grow up. For some of us, growing into maturity takes a lifetime of experience, and for others, like the brother who died before I ever met him, maturity comes in an instant. God brings us to Himself, let's us put aside the "childish things" of this life, and enter into His kingdom as the complete people He created us to be. I loved being a child, and it's cool being a young person today, but each day brings me a small measure of maturity, and another step closer to all that I'm meant to be. How good is that?

Dear friends, now we are children of God, and what we will be has not yet been made known   1 John 3: 2

Chapter Twenty Nine

Saying Good Bye

*A*fter the seventh grade I was used to high school life and the eighth grade was a breeze. I was beginning to pick up academically enough to really enjoy school and become friends with teachers and students alike. It was fun to arrive at the first day of school and actually go up to people I knew and felt comfortable with and start chatting and give them a hug. Finally I felt that I was known as Nicki and nothing else.

One event that may have colored my eighth grade was the fact that my grandma got sick and died and my parents had to both go off to America to the funeral. They seemed to be gone a long time and it was one of those times when you're a missionary kid and realize you're not like other kids, because in this case you can't just jump up and go home for a funeral, even if it IS your Grandmother. I felt really sad not to be there to say goodbye, but I guess I'd said goodbye the last time I saw her, and I know she'll always be in my heart.

This was another instance of being glad that Charity and I were such good friends, because I could stay with her while my parents were in the States, and she'd be there for me while I was sad. After awhile, my parents came home and the year was going well until my parents dropped the news on me that we might be moving.

Now when my parents say "might" it usually means that we are. I've learned that much after all these years of living with them. I have to say now that as I was almost 15, they were a little more open in discussing with me about the move and asking my opinion before they made up their minds, but I still felt a little surprised that we couldn't just keep living the dream in

Sydney. At first I did and said what any frustrated teen-ager would say if their parents told them that they were moving. One minute I would say "Yes Mom, I'm so happy I will have a good fresh start at another school". And then I would say in the next minute, "Mom and Dad, you're destroying my life!"

Now, I wasn't exactly too sure how to feel about the whole move but I guess in a way I was happy that I could have a fresh start, because I always like challeng-es, but then on the other hand, now that I finally had some good friends I hated the thought of leaving them. We were moving to the Gold Coast area near Brisbane because there are a lot of Japanese there for my par-ents to work with, but what about me? My brother wouldn't be going with us as he was in his last year of University, so how would I get along without him to tease me and drive me everywhere? I couldn't believe this was happening and I didn't know how to feel.

One day my mom called the school I'd be attending in the Gold Coast to see if I could get in, and they chatted a few minutes and in the process of the conversation, it was mentioned that a new Drama and Music wing was being opened in a couple of weeks with a big musical production. Too bad we wouldn't be there to see it.

168

Then suddenly, my Mom remembered she had some Frequent Flyer points and could get us some free plane tickets and before you knew it, she and I were on our way to see the school.

To our surprise, before the school even gave us a tour, they gave me an interview, looked over my records and announced that I was definitely accepted if I wanted to come. In Australia, private schools usually have long waiting lists, so this seemed like something from God. It was even more exciting that the principal mentioned in passing that he is the uncle of my favorite singer, Rebecca St. James! I showed him my purity ring that was on my finger and he was quite impressed as well. How ironic that my favorite singer would be his niece, so maybe that's what did it for me! Anyway, we walked out of the office accepted into the 9th grade and I hadn't even seen the school!

That night at the play, I was astounded with the talent and seeming love the students had for each other. It's hard to explain both wanting to be a part of such a great team, and being very overwhelmed at the same time with the events of the day. After the interview and the play that night, we had some time to kill the next day before our flight back to Sydney, so we thought we would start going in concentric circles from the school and check out rental houses. We would be moving up to the Gold Coast just a few days before school started so it would be nice to have a place to live.

We were surprised to find that the rental market was very tight, with people having to go on waiting lists and be interviewed to be accepted, so we were 'concerned' about the living situation, to say the least. As we drove 200 metres (about a block) from the school, I saw a basketball net on a house and asked my mom, "Mom, do you think God would give us a basket ball net?" I thought that would be great, because during the last year I had taken up basketball, but had no place to practice. Little did I know, as my mom smiled at me and mumbled something, that she was actually wondering if God would even give us a roof over our heads.

I'm glad she didn't quench my enthusiasm or my simple faith in God like some adults do when they've lived a lot of life. Anyway, we continued up the road for a few more houses and there was a beautiful white house. Mom looked up at it and it was for sale! While she was calling the real estate agent to find out how much, etc. her eyes fell on the mail box and she seemed very

170

agitated suddenly. As soon as she hung up with the realtor, she started crying and dialing Dad on the mobile. As it turned out, the number on the mail box had caught her attention because it was the same number of our house in Japan.

Then, as if that wasn't weird enough, just as she was starting to explain all this to Dad, I saw it! Down on the garage, half hidden by a tree, was a beautiful basketball net! God had answered my prayer in just the time it takes to drive a city block! I don't need to tell you that we were able to buy the house, and I walk every day just two blocks to school. God is so good.

That afternoon we caught our flight back to Sydney and at the end of the year packed up and said goodbye to everyone including my old school friends. As it was the last day of me being at Beachview Grammer the girls in my grade threw me a big surprise party and even the girls that didn't like me all through primary school showed up and even said they were sad to see me leave. Who knows if they were being truthful or not, but it felt good to know that I'd done my best with those situations and I accomplished what I wanted for my grade that year. I hope and pray that I taught them some compassion towards each other by my actions.

Think about it:

Don't give up! Throughout the seventh and eighth grade I was compelled to be a friend towards everyone, including the people I disliked. I was told to love the people I disliked and show them what a true friend is really like. I prayed for them and asked God to keep them safe. I felt weird praying for those that had treated me horribly but you know after a while, it felt really good. I felt like I was doing something for God and being kind to them. If you ever feel down, your friends are the best people that can help you. They comfort you and pray with you and tell you that it's going to be OK. The real best friend you'll ever have is Christ. He can show you to a place of joy and be a great friend. He knows how to listen to you and is there for you when you need him most.

Now I know in part; then I shall know fully, even as I am fully known   1 Corinthians 13:12

Chapter Thirty

Another New Beginning

*Y*es, it is yet another new beginning. From Armavir, Russia to Japan; from Japan to Australia with stops along the way in Hong Kong, Ethiopia and America. Now, from Sydney to the Gold Coast. As I thought about it, I was excited.

I'm going into ninth grade in a new school, with new challenges beckoning from every corner. The drama club is planning a huge production later this year, and I hope I can be in it. The music team at our new church is inviting me to come and join them.

So exciting, but could I do it? Well, if the first few weeks of school were any indication, then I didn't think I'd have anything to worry about. At my first day here, I had all the old familiar butterflies that I'd felt before, in so many places. I walked into the school grounds and started looking around at it this time not as a visitor, but as a student! Taking a deep breath and stepping into the school office, I was greeted at once by a kind lady named Jill. When I saw her smile I had a feeling that I was going to fit in very well here. I hadn't even met any of the students yet but by that smile I sensed that it was God telling me that it was going to be OK.

Jill walked me down to where several girls were standing and introduced me to them. They were all grade nine girls, which was a relief because I had no idea how I'd ever find the ninth grade classroom. One girl in particular seemed to have the biggest smile ever. Was it just my imagination or was everyone smiling at me that day? I introduced myself and started to get to know the girls. Right from that moment I felt that these girls were more accepting of me and I wondered if

174

I was going to have a better experience in this school. One beautiful girl stood out to me as she was the first one to come over and say hi and introduce herself. I saw her face and thought that I had seen it before, and then I remembered. I'd seen her speaking at church the week before. Also, I'd seen her picture in the newspaper! It seemed that she had been impacted immensely by the tragedy of the Boxing Day tsunami that had hit Thailand and Indonesia a few months before. In keeping with her outgoing personality, she really wanted to facilitate the recovery by sending school supplies to places and towns that had been washed away and badly need help. Somehow, even though she was barely thirteen, she had organized a big nationwide campaign to collect materials and resources and get them shipped to the most needy places. What she did, as a young girl, was really awesome and I could have been intimidated by so famous a person. However, within just a minute or two of talking to her, I realized that she was so kind and compassionate towards me, making me feel like I was in the right place at the right time. Maybe because of her love of helping others, instead of being awed and overwhelmed by her, I was made to feel that we'd known each other all our lives.

Jillian is an amazing girl. Since my first day she has

always greeted me in the morning as I arrive at school, with the biggest smile on her face as if to say, "It's me again and I want to make you feel happy today." Maybe someday she'll be writing a book about how God is working in her life as well. I'm sure it would be a best seller. Jillian and her friends have become my friends too. And wouldn't you know it? God was now leading me to another friend, from Japan.

Think about it:

I titled this chapter "A New Beginning", which is not really true, when you think about it. Every day of our lives is a new beginning, in that we haven't experienced it yet, but in another sense, every day is just a continuation of the day before. Everything I experience today will be seen and filtered based on who I am and what I'm becoming. Realizing that, I have a lot more confidence about the future. There may be things there that I haven't experienced yet, but I will be there, so it won't be totally unknown, will it? God is showing me new things every day, but He's letting me see those things through the eyes and the life that He's given me, and He's assuring me that, just as He's been with me in the past, He will be with me today and tommorrow, and in all the days to come. I like that.

A new command I give you: Love one another

John 13: 34

Chapter Thirty One

Reaching Out

a few weeks after my parents and I had settled into our new home, we started a Japanese Bible study. You see, every year, my high school, Hillcrest Christian College, gets several international exchange students, and many of them are Japanese. Because we can relate to being all alone in a foreign country, we wanted to reach out to them, so we started an after school get together for them.

This year, there was a new Japanese student who had come to our school and the first time I saw her, I knew that she and I had something in common. She was looking confused and lonely, but instead of dealing with it by being hyperactive, like I used to be, she had drawn into herself, looking very black and moody. I tried to think of how I could make her feel welcome.

Her name was Nao, and she was staying with a Christian family, going to our church every Sunday and attending school as well. It must be hard on the students to come from a totally non-English speaking background and be thrown into a completely new language situation, especially where no one understands Japanese, much less speaks it. I remembered how it felt when I came from Russia and my heart went out to her.

Soon after she arrived, it began to be whispered around that she was from a rough background and had a lot of problems with her family back in Japan. She preferred a punk look, which only drew trouble at my school, because of the strict dress codes. She was struggling with the new language and all the adjustments to living in a new family, and it was becoming obvious that she had started feeling as if she was worth nothing. I didn't know it, but she was begging to be sent home
178

and believe me, the teachers were ready. My mom kept saying, "If Nao goes back to Japan, that's the end of her, because what she really needs is Jesus. My Mom even went into school a few times to encourage them not to give up on Nao.

One day, as I was thinking about the things I had to do that day, I decided to speak to her and see if I could be of some help. We had decided to start a 'girl's time out' at our house for these lonely international students, and I thought maybe she'd like to come. I walked up to her and surprised even myself by speaking in perfect "kid" Japanese to her. She was surprised that I was even speaking to her and a few moments later finally realized that I was speaking in Japanese. Her face lit up as she looked at the big smile on my face, and she began jabbering away in her Osaka-based Japanese, which was a lot different than the Japanese I remembered, but I was able to follow along. From that day we began to greet each other every day and spend a few minutes just chatting, although not at a very deep level, I was sad to say.

At my school we have Chapel, or a mini church service every week or so. Some people love it, and others look at it as a chance to rest or goof off. On this particular day, as we all sat in our strictly appointed rows during the all school chapel, I noticed that during the service Nao had started to cry. I was sad that she was sad, and thought about what I could do to help her. I saw a teacher heading for her, so I thought if I could slip unobtrusively out of my seat and could get to her first, I would just take her outside quickly before she got in trouble yet again. As soon as we escaped, I sat her down and said to her in Japanese, "Nao, don't cry. You need to listen to me. You are an amazing girl and God loves you... and so do I." The look on her face of astonishment thru her tears led me to believe that she hadn't heard that too often, but I believed it to be true. Jesus always found the hurting and the injured and could somehow see through the scars to the beautiful hearts.

I basically got the message across somehow with my weird Japanese that she needed to accept Jesus Christ as her Savior. After I explained that to her, she just looked at me and started nodding her head as if she knew exactly what I was talking about. Now, I was a little surprised because I was wondering where all my Japanese was coming from. I hadn't spoken in Japanese for such a long time, but knowing the Lord works in astonishing ways. I prayed real hard and looked at

Nao again, but this time I looked deep into her eyes.

"Nao, you look like you can't survive this without God, do you want to become a Christian?"

I repeated that about twice. I have no idea what I said but God just started putting words into my mouth. As I started talking to her, I started praying harder and harder. It settled her down and she stopped crying and looked at me. I kept praying real earnestly, all the while speaking to Nao and convincing her that she needed to become a Christian right then and there. I was working so hard at convincing her that she needed God and all the while she was just politely waiting for me to stop talking so she could accept Christ! Maybe, as I think about it now, I needed to actually believe what I was praying and relax and let God do His work, because before I knew it, Nao prayed a beautiful prayer to become a Christian that day, using words and ideas that she could have only received from God, because I didn't have the language ability to put those words in her mouth or her heart!

The experience that day may have made a difference in Nao's life, but I know for sure that my own life was changed. I saw in those few minutes that this was what God had created me for: to go to people in need. I remembered my Dad saying that one of my yochien teachers back in Japan had commented that I "always went to the kids who were crying." I believe now that it was a part of what God placed in my heart from the very beginning. He put me in impossible circumstances, then pulled me out with His own miraculous strength, and in the process said, "This, My child, is what you are to do: go to those who are in impossible circumstances. Find the needy, the suffering, the crying. Reach out to them with My Words. I will use you to bring a hope and a future to people sitting in darkness. I did it for you; I will do it for them."

It wasn't just those words and the act of Nao dedicating her life to God that made me want to serve God by being a comfort and guide towards non Christians. I'll have to say it was also the impact that my ninth grade English teacher has had on my life. From the first day I met her she's helped me through so much. One day she gave me a poem about struggling and it made me realize that I wasn't the only person in our world that has faced struggles throughout their life. I have found Mrs. Henn an inspiration because she's using her talent to teach her students and some how impact their lives, creating for them an atmosphere of truth and love.
182

She taught me a lot during the ninth grade, including helping me to see how my identity is one of the most important things in life. As long as I am a Christian I can cling to that identity and then just relax, knowing that God is in control. Sure, life has brought me a few hardships and challenges, but there has always been God watching over me and people along the way to give me compassion and love.. I guess all I can say now is "thank you".

Think about it:

When I think back now to that yochien teacher's comment that I was "always going to the children who are crying", I wonder, was she inspired by God to say that, or was it just an observation that I've since tried to live up to? Either way, that comment has gone a long way toward helping me discover my own purpose and call from God. That fact makes me really want to be careful about what I say about people, since my words can do a lot toward moving a person in one direction or another.

Epilogue

$\mathcal{J}$ had just had my sixteenth birthday. In America this is always a big deal. Here in Australia, your eighteenth seems to be the one they focus on, but my Mom and Dad said, "Hey! You're Australian AND American; why not celebrate both? They ordered special "Sweet Sixteen" decorations from America, and my brother even came up from Sydney to be the "DJ" at my party.

He brought along his new girlfriend who would soon become his fiancee', so I knew it was pretty special. I'll never forget that night. Every one of my sixteen carefully selected guests came formally dressed and we had a beautiful evening, eating and listening to music. Everywhere there were glittering stars hanging and white fairys lights twinkling. I thought of all the beautiful stars back in Ethiopia, and the beautiful music I've experienced through the years. I thought of all the friends I've had, starting with the orphanage and the lovely Dr. Vegislav. I remembered the good times and the difficult times, and realized that my first sixteen years have truly been a gift from God. Life has been so very good to me. I have a family that loves me, school friends, and a purpose to live for.

Mom and Dad let me know from the start that my "special" Bible verse was Jeremiah 29:11, but I didn't really understand why until I finished writing this book. The story goes all the way back to the day of my birth, and now that I think about it, before then, even. You've had a glimpse of some of the interesting things that have happened to me along the way but let's look again to that morning on August 9th, 1993:

Tony positioned himself on the deck this cool summer morning. It was August 9th, 1993. Today would be 'Nicki's first birthday with her new family. She had come to the Woods' family the October before, learned not one but two new and completely different languages, forgetting most of the original one. She'd had surgery and could now see as straight as an arrow.

Her paternal grandparents had come to Japan to finally meet her and had a riotous good time showing her the wonders of the world and laughing at her funny mix of expressions and languages.

Later today, she would have her first ever birthday party at the age of 4.

Tony settled in his chair and opened his Bible, the "Thru the Bible" version that he had laid aside years before. As he had been cleaning out his office one day, he'd noticed it languishing on the shelf and had decided to read through it again this year.

He took a sip of his coffee, looked again at the beautiful sunrise and opened the Bible up to the August 9th reading. There on the margin was some faded red ink and the date, August 9, 1989. He almost choked in surprise, because as we all now know, that was THE DAY that Nicki had been born in far away Russia! And what was the verse he had underlined?

Jeremiah 29:11... *For I know the plans I have for you, saith the Lord, Plans to prosper you and not to harm you, plans to give you hope and a future.*

Thank you, Lord, for showing me the truth of that passage. Thank you for the plans you have for me, and for your promise that they will not be used to hurt me, but to give me all the hope and joy the future can bring.

Amen

Other books from Marton Publishing

Uncle Buddy ISBN 0-9749-8411-6
by Tony R Woods
Paperback Retail US$5.75 plus shipping

From the small West Texas town of San Angelo to the heart of Africa, Buddy Woods is living testimony to God's work and purpose in the lives of His people. Follow that exciting trail in this biographical sketch of the man who has become known around the world simply as "Uncle Buddy"

The Road Rising ISBN 0-9749841-2-4
by Tony R Woods
Hardback Retail US$29.95 plus shipping
Paperback Version US$21.95
Japanese Versions also available

Through the daily journal of a backpacker known only as "Friend", follow the seeker's path on a one-year adventure beset by fire, flood and the demonic power of the Evil Man. Survival depends upon the phenomenon known as "Rendezvous", a place where fellow travelers gather to discover the depth of love which is available from the One Who called them to the journey.

Leaving the Trail ISBN 0-9749841-9-1
by Tony R Woods
Paperback Retail US$19.95 plus shipping

The story of Fisher and Sandy, whom we met in The Road Rising. Beginning their journey as husband and wife, they are soon called to a new and exciting challenge: to seek out those who have lost the way. Departure from the established trail lead the young couple to a horror so unspeakable that they can only move forward in faith, depending upon God for His protection and wisdom.

Looking for a Lamb ISBN 0-9749841-4-0
by Tony R Woods
Hardback Retail US$16.95 plus shipping
Japanese Version also available

An allegorical look at Christian grief recovery, from the pages of a father who endured the agonizing death of his first born son to leukemia. Reminiscent of the biblical story of Abraham and Isaac, both fathers encounter sacrificial lambs on their way to the mountain top. But it is not until they reach the summit that they find the True Lamb and lasting answers to the questions which haunt them.

On the Road With John ISBN 0-9749841-6-7
by Tony R Woods
Spiral Bound Retail US$9.95 plus shipping
Japanese Version also available

Based on the "ROAD" method (Read, Observe, Apply, Discuss), this
look at the Fourth Gospel is designed for either individuals or small
groups, divided into 52 sections for a one year weekly Bible study.

Beasts of Iron ISBN 0-9749841-8-3
by Paul Goosen
Paperback Retail US$26.95 plus shipping

Number One in the "Nether Realm Novel" series by author Paul
Goosen, this science fiction adventure will take you to a realm ruled
by the beast, and survived by man. "Welcome to Earth ... or what's
left of it"

For book orders or inquiries, contact Marton Publishing:

Suite 249/51
Locked Bag 1
Robina Town Centre QLD
Australia   4230

or:

Marton Publishing LLC
350 Greenbriar Trail
Holly Lake Ranch TX
USA   75765

or by email:

martonpub@optusnet.com.au

And don't forget...

"Sydney-based Nathan Tasker is a man with a mission. Like most singer-songwriters, he is keen to tell his lyrical stories to all who will listen. For almost a decade, he has been working towards perfecting his craft. He has recorded seven albums and has performed at more than 1500 concerts. Sales of his recorded product total over 22 000 units.

"The past two years have seen Nathan's star continue to rise with consistent Australian success. With five top ten radio singles, including a number one and nation-wide press and media coverage, Nathan is the premier male Christian artist. To cap it all off, Nathan was awarded Pacific Songwriter of the Year 2005 – top honours in the Southern Hemispheres most lucrative mainstream songwriting competition.

"And above it all, threaded through his material, is the timeless message of God's love for mankind. The "greatest story ever told" is an integral part of Nathan Tasker's story."

From his website: www.nathantasker.com